# THE HUNGRY BRAIN

# In A Nutshell
### s e r i e s

# THE HUNGRY BRAIN

## The Nutrition/Cognition Connection

In A Nutshell

collection

## Susan Augustine

CORWIN
A SAGE Company

*For information:*

Corwin
A SAGE Company
2455 Teller Road
Thousand Oaks, California 91320
(800) 233-9936
Fax: (800) 417-2466
www.corwinpress.com

SAGE Ltd.
1 Oliver's Yard
55 City Road
London EC1Y 1SP
United Kingdom

SAGE India Pvt. Ltd.
B 1/I 1 Mohan Cooperative
  Industrial Area
Mathura Road,
  New Delhi 110 044
India

SAGE Asia-Pacific Pte. Ltd.
33 Pekin Street #02-01
Far East Square
Singapore 048763

Printed in the United States of America

A catalog record of this book is available from the Library of Congress.

ISBN: 978-0-9763-4263-2

This book is printed on acid-free paper.

09   10   11   12   13   10   9   8   7   6   5   4   3   2   1

# Contents

# Preface

Imagine an average child, someone who seems perfectly normal. A child who blends in so well that others believe she is a happy, healthy little girl. Yet, this child feels uncontrollable, uncomfortable depression, a feeling so mystifying, so perplexing, the human intellect seems unable to comprehend or even respond.

I was that child and that was the first half of my life, consumed with feelings of pain. I believed dying was better than living. In fact, I hoped I would die. I even tried to die. I thought other kids seemed happy and able to handle life, but I felt I could not. Even psychiatric help and a program of various drug therapies did not help. Finally, I tried to end the pain with a suicide attempt.

My depression lasted 22 years. Then, I met a physician who diagnosed my condition as a biochemical depression. He began to balance my brain chemistry with nutrients. I stopped eating sugary foods, which exacerbated my already delicate chemistry. I took vitamins and minerals and focused on a low sugar diet. Within two weeks I felt different. In fact, I remember the moment I no longer felt depressed. It was a Friday. I felt the normal exhaustion of a working week completed, but for the first time I did not feel melancholy in any way. No sadness! I thought to myself, "I think I feel happy. I think this is what happy feels like". It was the first time I did not experience the darkness of not wanting to be alive. Its absence was so noticeable, it was as though a throbbing music had finally stopped. I was 22 years old at the time. Now, well, let's just say I am no longer in my 20s. But I am happy and well.

Because of my experience, I have been studying nutrition and its effects on mood, mind, memory, and behavior for more than 20 years. This is why I wrote this book.

■ □ ■ □ ■

# Introduction

Presented in this book for educators is a new concept that breaks from the traditions in which teachers think about the brain and how children learn. It's food first this time. It is time to feed the brain, literally! The importance of good nutrition to good health cannot be denied. Yet, we have simply ignored this fact in schools. The brain, even more so than other organs in the body, does not eat with impunity.

The word diet comes from the Greek word, diatia, which means, a way of life. This applies to all of life's eating, including brain food or brain nutrition. Unfortunately eating for "brain gain" is not very well modeled in our schools!

Since the brain is the busiest organ in the body, working even as we sleep, it requires a vast amount of nutrients flowing through it moment by moment to function optimally. This means that nutrients in the form of amino acids from proteins, vitamins and minerals from plant foods, specific fats from foods, and glucose in the form of blood sugar are needed by this busy brain. Furthermore, there is no room in the brain to store food up for a rainy day. Learners must eat nutritious foods daily for peak brain performance. When the brain fuel supply plummets it's difficult for people to concentrate and to remember.

## Three Food Groups

In order to simplify the teaching of nutrition, this author has comprised three food groups. Do not be fooled by the truncated version of the famous Food Pyramid. In this author's experience of teaching nutrition to teachers and children, it was noted that kids, and even adults, often cannot make sense of the Food Pyramid. Nor did they care to.

The three food groups are comprehensive and easy enough for children to remember. Truly, all foods do fall into only three classifications: animal foods, plant foods and junk foods, the last category having little or no food value.

The brain prefers good clean unadulterated foods from the plant and animal groups. If it grows in the ground, or we pick it off of a vine or tree, it's a plant. If it is walking around on four legs or two legs (fowl), or if it swims in the ocean or lake, it is considered an animal or animal food.

If it is manufactured in a factory from scraps of food or food artifacts with much added sugar, salt, fat and fake flavors and colors, it's a junk food and should be avoided as much as humanly possible. Candies, cookies, cakes, fake salty snacks, such as Cheetos, are all considered junk food. Many breakfast cereals contain fake bits of so called food (such as marshmallows) and lots of added sugar. They are most definitely junk foods. These foods can wreak havoc on the brain by robbing it of nutrition in two ways: (1) too much sugar robs the brain and body of chromium, a mineral important for brain functioning; and (2) by crowding out room for the more nutritious foods the brain really needs. When a child is consuming too much junk food there is no room in the stomach for healthier, real food that has nutritional value. Our western world has become so impervious to the glut of junk food that exists that we no longer think it strange or unusual to consume a liter of soda per day instead of water. Moreover, a lunch of cream cheese (fake food) on a bagel, a meal so stripped of nutrients that laboratory rats have literally perished on it is seen as the norm.

> If it is manufactured in a factory from scraps of food or food artifacts with much added sugar, salt, fat and fake flavors and colors, it's a junk food and should be avoided as much as humanly possible.

# THREE FOOD GROUPS

## Plant Foods

Fruits

Nuts (raw and unsalted)

Berries

Rice

Oats

Wild rice

Beans

Sprouts

Buckwheat

Vegetables

Seeds

Leaves (lettuce)

Whole wheat

Millet

Legumes

Peas

Potatoes

Sea vegetables

## Animal Foods

Eggs

Chicken

Beef

Lamb

Buffalo

Cheese

Fish

Turkey

Pork

Venison

Milk

Sour cream

## Junk Foods

Candies

Pies

Cakes

Coffee cake

Corn chips (most, not all)

Soft drinks

Cookies

Ice-cream

Doughnuts

Potato chips

Gum

# Brain Food

Which foods does the brain require to function optimally? The answer to that question is enclosed in the food groups one and two: plant and animal foods, with plant foods being first. Plant foods contain all the important nutrients for survival, repair, and re-growth. People who choose to consume only plant foods must know how to eat enough of a variety of plant foods to receive enough protein. Proteins are very important for the hungry brain.

# Protein and the Brain

> Amino acids are the basic units of growth, and are also essential for brain function.

The word "protein" is derived from the Greek word *prote~in*, which means, "of first importance". Proteins contain 20 or more amino acids, of which eight are considered essential, meaning that they must be eaten daily. Two are semi-essential for adults but essential for children. Amino acids are the basic units of growth, and are also essential for brain function. Amino acids build proteins.

> Most people seem to need about 20 to 30 grams of protein three times per day.

Without amino acids from proteins, our brain cannot produce and feel optimistic, calm, enthusiastic, or comforted. The neurotransmitters, which are chemical brain messengers, send out all these positive feelings. We now know that these good feelings affect learning. However, the manufacturing of these very important brain chemicals can be made only by consuming proteins that contain amino acids (more on neurotransmitters later). The more protein the better for the brain, especially in the morning! Most people seem to need about 20 to 30 grams of protein three times per day.

When we eat proteins, more norepinephrine and dopamine are available than serotonin. That is because tyrosine and phenylalanine, which yield dopamine and norepinephrine, are more plentiful in protein foods than tryptophan. Norepinephrine and dopamine are the alertness neurotransmitters. Serotonin is the mellow, or feel good, neurotransmitter. Norepinephrine, dopamine and serotonin are all neurotransmitters; tyrosine, tryptophan and phenylalanine are amino acids.

> It might be helpful to think of proteins (containing amino acids) as food for thinking and carbohydrates as food for drowsiness.

Tyrosine, tryptophan, and phenylalanine all compete for delivery to the brain, and tryptophan, being less concentrated, loses out. Even when foods high in the amino acid tryptohpan are eaten, tyrosine and phenylalanine will win for entrance into the brain. (Turkey and dairy products are examples of foods that are high in tryptophan.) Tryptophan will be picked up more readily by the brain when carbohydrate foods are eaten along with the protein.

Amino acids from proteins also function in other ways that are just as important to brain function as neurotransmitters. They make up the enzymes that regulate neurotransmitters. Enzymes assist in neuronal-receiving, processing, interpreting, and putting out vital information. It might be helpful to think of proteins (containing amino acids) as food for thinking and carbohydrates as food for drowsiness. You will read more about proteins in chapters 1 and 2.

> Fruits, vegetables, nuts, seeds and whole grains contain the vitamins the brain needs.

## Vitamins and the Brain

Vita comes from the Old French word, *vital*, which means life. Indeed, vitamins promote life in the brain. The vitamins are the co-enzymes, meaning they are essential for the manufacturing of all of the neurotransmitters that are mentioned above. Most of today's processed food is depleted of these essential vitamins. Fruits, vegetables, nuts, seeds and whole grains contain the vitamins the brain needs.

# Minerals and the Brain

Minerals, too, are co-enzymes, meaning they are essential for proper brain function. Some functions of minerals include: activation of neural communications, regulation of brain metabolism, and protection of the brain from certain toxins.

> Minerals are obtained primarily from vegetables and grains and some flesh foods.

Minerals are obtained primarily from vegetables and grains and some flesh foods.

You will read more about vitamins and minerals in Chapter 2.

# Fats and the Brain

Fats help everything run smoothly. And, since the busy, hungry brain is 60% fat, Chapter 4 tells us more on the importance of the fats for the brain. There is a special fat that the brain favors. And then there are fats that have a deleterious effect on the brain.

# Water and the Brain

Picture the dehydrated individual who wanders the desert. He hallucinates about a water-well. There, he may quench his avid thirst. Alas, it's just a mirage.

In our every day life, however, water is a quick fix for the mind that needs constant replenishment to survive, just like the weary traveler. As with the rest of the body, the brain works best when it is hydrated. The brain consists of about 78% water.

Athletes provide more practical data about the brain's need for water. Vigorous movement in the heat of the day can create excessive sweat. Losses of up to two liters of fluid an hour may occur and mount rapidly – more rapidly than can be replaced. As observed in athletes competing in hot, humid climates, brain activity is highly sensitive to dehydration. The body compensates with less than one liter per hour at best (Pawlak, 2005). A fluid loss of less than 2% can imbalance the athlete's brain chemicals, resulting in mental confusion, irrational statements and loss of coordination and balance.

Water can be an easy addendum to any classroom or school!

> The brain works best when it is hydrated.

# Exercise and the Brain

Included in *The Hungry Brain* is a chapter on exercise (Chapter 6), for good reason. Children who move do better in school (Diamond, 1998). One of the reasons for this is that exercise delivers oxygen to all of the cells, including brain cells. All cells need oxygen. But many urban children have no time during the school day for any physical activity if it is not a gym day. There is no outdoor recess due to the safety issues of being outside.

Another good reason for exercise is that the road to overeating is paved with inactivity. According to *Physical Activity and Health: A Report of the Surgeon General* (1996), " inactive people are twice as likely to have symptoms of depression" than more active people.

## DID YOU KNOW?

The road to overeating is paved with inactivity. According to *Physical Activity and Health: A Report of the Surgeon General* (1996), "inactive people are twice as likely to have symptoms of depression" than more active people.

# Chapter 1

# Where's the Food?

*Every novel idea passes through three stages.*
*First, people say it isn't true. Then they say it is true but not important. And finally, they say it is true and important, but not new.*

*— anonymous*

If our great-grandparents could see the meals we eat today, they might ask, "Where's the food?". Unfortunately, fresh, unadulterated cooking appears to have gone the way of horse-drawn carriages. Today, most children are brought up on processed foods that lack many of the essential nutrients needed by growing bodies and developing brains. Popular processed foods claim all but 10 cents of our grocery dollar.

Processed foods are those that have been altered, refined, overcooked, chemically treated, and stripped of nutrients. The primary purpose of these alternations is to create foodstuffs that can be sold to satisfy modern preferences for sweets and fats – tastes acquired by consumers who are acclimated to modern foods' unhealthy ingredients. And so the question "where's the food?" seems especially relevant as our modern diet bears little resemblance to the nutrient-rich foods our great grandparents ate years ago.

> Popular processed foods claim all but 10 cents of our grocery dollar.

The loss of real food began food by food, year by year beginning at various points in time during the 19th century. For example, prior to the introduction of processed foods on a mass basis, ice-cream was not only a special, but also a wholesome, treat. Whole eggs, milk, and sugar were cranked together by hand, comprising the delicious ingredients for this cold, smooth mixture. Its very preparation marked a cause for celebration. People who prepared and ate ice-cream usually shared in a mutually enjoyable experience among family and friends.

Although ice-cream still ranks as one of our favorite things to eat, today it no longer resembles the naturally delicious concoction prepared by our great-grandparents. The whole eggs, milk, and sugar of the ice-cream of yesterday have given way to the following list of ingredients commonly found in ice-cream today:

- Diethyl glucol: A cheap chemical used as an emulsifier instead of eggs. It's the same chemical used in paint remover and antifreeze.

- Piperohal: A substitute for vanilla. This is widely used by exterminators to kill lice.

- Aldehyde C17: Used to convey a cherry flavor. This is an inflammable liquid used in anline dyes, plastics and rubber.

- Ethyl acetate: Used to suggest a pineapple flavor. It is also a cleaner for leather and textile. Its vapors have caused chronic lung and liver problems.

## White versus Natural

We didn't always ingest food loaded with artificial chemicals; in almost all cases, we developed our bad habits over time. Bread has been a major part of the human diet from the earliest times of human food preparation, and is considered one of nature's almost-perfect foods. However, beginning in Victorian England, individual preferences for bread varieties developed some less-than-healthy tendencies that began to cross class and economic lines. Clean-looking, white refined bread was preferred by the middle and upper classes while dark, uneven-textured whole wheat bread was identified with lower class tastes. Little did the upper classes realize, however, that the refinement process for white bread would bring about a loss of valuable nutrients needed for healthy eating. White bread required discarding the wheat berry's outer layer – bran – and its vital heart – the germ – leaving nothing behind but the starchy center and significant reductions in valued nutrients: 97% of thiamine, 66% of riboflavin, 94% of pyridoxine, 27% of protein, 57% of pantothenic acid, and 86% of niacin. With the advent of just this one process, therefore, a food once rich in nutrients became nutritionally bankrupt for generations to come.

## Nutrients Lost

Present-day flour refining is a highly-sophisticated process that involves the adding of fillers, binders and texturizers to extend shelf life, and alter the appearance of the product. Beginning with the essence of bread itself, modern wheat has been designed to produce an energy food rather than offer a balance of nutrients naturally found in the seed. The essential oil content of modern wheat is naturally low, about 5%. But by the time the flour has been purified, it has been reduced to 1.5%. With the reduction in essential oil, Vitamin E is lost. Natural whole grain bread contains ten times as much Vitamin E as does refined white bread.

During the Industrial Revolution food-processing methods began to change even further. Sugar, flour and rice were next to undergo modern alterations through the refinement process. Just as white bread was now preferred by middle and upper income people, white rice and sugar were beginning to become the same group's designer varieties of choice, thus dramatically reducing the nutrients previously available via unrefined versions of these foods.

■ ☐ ■ ☐ ■

## Breakfast in a Box

Another change in food preparation occurred in the mid-1850s with the creation of new foods to incorporate white refined sugar. William R. Kellogg, brother of Dr. John Harvey Kellogg, initiated a series of experiments to produce a new type of breakfast food, cereal. Around 1890, Kellogg's Corn Flakes™ were officially launched in Battle Creek, Michigan (Levenstein, 1988). At around the same time, a real estate promoter by the name of Charles W. Post entered the food market with his grain-based drink, "Postem", naming it in honor of the founder. Using Kellogg's idea as a springboard, Post began to produce Grape Nuts™, another ready-to-eat cereal that gained immediate popularity with consumers. Shortly afterwards, 40 other imitations hit the store shelves, all incorporating sugar into the formula of the cereals. Since women, before the invention of the corn flake, were required to light a wood-burning stove to prepare meat or bacon for breakfast, the appeal of a no-fuss early meal was instant and overwhelming. Soon packages of cereal were popping up in kitchens across the country. Since then, eating packaged breakfast has become a universal American morning behavior, as the entrepreneurs of the breakfast business almost single-handedly have changed the way we eat.

## Processing Perfected

By 1900, the American food-processing industry had become very big business, with 20% of the country's manufacturing activity represented by food-processing alone. Canning, originally devised in France, was perfected and made popular by the famous entrepreneur Henry J. Heinz (Levenstein, 1988). The twin forces of brand-name appeal and hard-sell marketing approaches were endorsed by retailers and manufacturers such as Kellogg, Borden, Swift, and Armour, who all understood the economics of mass production. The mass production of food continues to serve as the engine for the way we eat today.

## Habituation Havoc

Just as our food supply has drastically changed since the days of our great grandparents, so have the diseases we die from. The major killers of the late 20th century include coronary heart disease, cancer and diabetes. It has become apparent that many of these now-prevalent degenerative diseases are not caused by simple viral infections, but by a combination of variables that produce a breakdown in the efficiency of the defensive mechanisms of the human body, including the brain. What does this have to do with the developing brains of our children? Everything, from the psychological to the physiological. Let's start with the psychological first.

The question always asked of nutritionists – "How bad is junk food?" – is not the only one to ask. You could also ask, "What's missing from junk food?"

Just think seriously about junk food for a moment. We all know children who seem to live on processed foods almost exclusively. But are their growing bodies getting adequate amounts of nutrients required for their unique nutritional needs? Are their busy brains being fed the appropriate foods to ensure efficient metabolic functions? As our grandparents might ask in looking at our children's eating habits – "Where's the food?" – the answers lie in the brain's need for certain kinds of food to perform its important work.

### DID YOU KNOW?

A famous Gallup poll was conducted in September of 1989. Americans were called and asked what they were having for dinner. Fifty percent of the people polled replied that they were having "frozen, packaged or take-out meals."

The busy brain controls the entire body. Sections of the brain are responsible for controlling such functions as thinking, hormones, involuntary movements, motor activity and sensory perception. These awesome tasks depend upon the brain's ability to properly metabolize food into usable forms of energy. The proper manufacture of energy in the brain also relies upon an adequate supply of the helper substances, vitamins and minerals. The brain depends more on adequate levels of nutrients than any other organ in the body.

In 1970, Americans spent about $6 billion on fast food; in 2000, they spent more than $110 billion. Americans now spend more money on fast food than on higher education, personal computers, computer software or new cars (Schlossor, 2001). Moreover, the foods eaten today are often so overly processed that in some cases they hardly resemble food. Take pretzels. Many children love to snack on them. That would be okay if they were made from whole wheat, which contains protein, fiber, Vitamin E, and the entire family of B vitamins. But because they come from refined wheat, they have very little nutritional value. With the exception of fiber, all of the above nutrients are necessary for brain functioning, with fiber being important for digestion, disease prevention, and protection of the gums.

---

### DID YOU KNOW?

In 1970, Americans spent about $6 billion on fast food; in 2000, they spent more than $110 billion. Americans now spend more money on fast food than on higher education, personal computers, computer software, or new cars (Schlossor, 2001).

---

■ □ ■ □ ■

**BRAIN JOGGER**

Have your students sit in pairs. One person will be the timer and the other the thinker. The thinker has 30 seconds to name all of the fast food restaurants he or she can think of in the 30-second time frame.

Switch roles.

Now have the pairs name vegetables in the 30-second time frame.

Which role was easier?

Now have them name as many brand name foods that come in a can.

Now have them list as many fruits and vegetables they have eaten in the past three days.

Compare and contrast lists.

# BRAIN FOOD LESSONS

# The Grapes of Rapp

## A Primary Level Lesson

## About Grapes

Grapes are berries, which grow on a woody vine. The botanical name for grapes is *Vitis vinifera*, which in Latin means "the vine that bears wine." More than two-thirds of the world's grapes are grown for wine, about 20% for table use, 10% are dried, and 1% are used for fruit juice. The volume of U.S. grape production ranks only under that of apples and oranges, with California producing the bulk of the crop. After almonds, grapes are California's largest food export.

## Nutritional Value

Grapes contain vitamins A, B-complex, and C. They also contain potassium and other trace minerals. Scientists are still unraveling the numerous benefits of grapes. Grapes contain some of the most powerful antioxidants (phytochemicals) known today. These antioxidants are proanthocyanadins, resveratrol, and polyphenols. Because grapes are a plant food, they contain necessary fiber.

A few years back, scientists discovered a phenomenon that they dubbed the French paradox. They found that while the French ate almost four times as much butter and three items as much lard, had higher cholesterol and blood pressure, and smoked just as much as Americans, they were two and a half times less likely to have a heart attack than Americans. Part of the French secret to heart health, researchers believe, is red wine, which of course is made from grapes. Most of the important compounds in the grape are found in the seed, the skin and the pulp. These are the parts we eat.

Grapes also contain another important phytochemical called ellagic acid. Ellagic acid is a cancer fighter. Ellagic acid is a unique scavenger of carcinogens. The resveratrol is unique to the skin of purple grapes and give grapes great prestige among the cancer fighters. Resveratrol has prevented cancer in animal and in cells grown in test tubes. Red and purple grapes contain many more nutrients than do green grapes.

Red grapes are especially high in nutritional value. They contain a higher nutritional value than green grapes. The skins of the purple grapes contain resveratrol, which is a newly discovered nutrient (phytochemical) that helps combat cancer. Grapes are filled with anti-cancer agents. The seeds of the grapes contain one of the most potent cancer fighting agents known today. These are called proanthocyainidins.

## Focus Activity

Ask the class if anyone ate something that came from a grape yesterday. See if they know what other foods come from grapes besides grape juice. Ask any of them if they know why grapes are so nutritious. Discuss what "nutritional value" means. Talk about what you can make with grapes (grape juice, grape pie, grape jam).

## Activity

Place students in groups of three. Assign the roles of:

- recorder
- material manager
- timer.

Have the material managers come and get four boxes of raisins, one sheet of newsprint and several crayons or markers. They are not to open their box of raisins until the teacher says it is time to do so.

The teacher holds up a box of raisins and has each group estimate how many raisins are in each box. The teacher samples the groups for their estimates. Now the material managers may open their group's box (just open one box at this point). The teacher explains that the material manager will open one box, then peek in it without dumping the raisins out, and estimate how many raisins are in each box. The recorder will write down the groups estimate on a piece of paper, along with your reasoning. Be prepared to share the reasoning with the class.

Sample each group, making certain that they explain their reasons for the estimation. Now, as a group, you may count the raisins. Record your answer. See how many groups came close to their estimation. Each individual member may now have their own box of raisins. Have them spill them on a piece of paper and arrange them in such a way that we can easily see how many you have (when you see that they are arranging them in arrays – talk about arrays and use that term from now on). Ask for a show of hands as to how many students are using arrays to count their raisins. Grouping by five or three will be a common response.

Before the teacher asks the student to give the number of raisins in their box, list the numbers from 20 to 50 on the board. The teacher is to tally each students' response. Which number appeared the most often? The number that appeared most often is called the mode. You can also have the students find the average number.

The teacher can hold up another box of raisins that has not been opened yet. "Based on the numbers written on the board, how many raisins do you think are in this box?" Give each group time to discuss it among themselves. Now sample each group.

They will most likely rely on the mode.

At this time the students may eat the nutritional raisins. Review some of the nutrients that raisins possess.

On the first sheet of newsprint have the students tell the story of their estimations. Write some words on the board to get them thinking. Write: array, mode, mean, guess, estimation, fiber, Vitamin A, B-complex vitamins, antioxidants, phytochemicals, resveratrol, polyphenols, ellagic acid, grape juice, jam, raisins, dehydrated.

The recorder is the person who writes the story on the first sheet of newsprint. The timer will give the group 15 minutes for this task. Have the materials manager read the groups story at the end of the 15 minutes. Display the stories around the room.

On the second sheet of paper have the groups write a song, rap or poem to try to convince others to eat more grapes and raisins because of their great nutritional value! Play the song *I Heard It Through The Grapevine*, for fun background music.

Ask each student to estimate how many times a month they will eat grapes or raisins. For bonus points or extra credit, have each group create a tally-sheet for the next month, and have a parent or guardian sign it each time they eat grapes, raisins, or drink real grape juice. Grape-flavored liquids and other sugary drinks do not count as real grape juice.

## Reflection

Why are grapes such a good value food? What did you learn about estimating? How many times next month do you think you will eat grapes or grape products? Frozen grapes make a good snack. Are you willing to try them?

# Cool Dude

## Intermediate and Middle School Lesson

## Focus Activity

Place the students in groups of three. Have them read the following passage about cucumbers together. After reading the following passage, have them formulate three questions to ask another group about cucumbers.

## About Cucumbers

Cucumbers contain over 90% water (more than any other food except watermelon). This water keeps its internal temperature several degrees cooler than the surrounding atmosphere. This is where we get the cliché "as cool as a cucumber." Cucumbers belong to the Cucurbitaceae family. This food family also includes pumpkin, cantaloupe, summer squash, winter squash and honeydew melons. Cucumbers are plentiful year round in most states. In winter, supplies come from California, Texas and Florida. Imported from Mexico and the Caribbean during the winter, cucumbers are usually waxed to prevent moisture loss during shipping and when in storage. The wax can be easily removed through peeling.

Cucumbers contain a digestive enzyme, erepsin, that breaks down protein, cleanses the intestines, and helps expel intestinal parasites, especially tapeworms (Wood, 1999). Cucumbers are a superior source of silicon, which is integral for calcium absorption. Silicon also helps reduce cholesterol, and it strengthens the nerve and heart tissue. Cucumbers, like all vegetables, are an excellent source of fiber. Fiber is important for gum, bowel and artery integrity. Fiber has been shown to lower blood cholesterol, keep blood sugar stable, and to keep some cancers at bay. Cucumbers are fat free and low in calories.

## Activity

In groups of three, have the students brainstorm as many different ways to eat cucumbers they can think of, using only nice healthful combinations of other terrific foods. Have them record their ideas on a large piece of chart paper. Have the groups each name their chart using only the letters in the word "cucumbers" to create the name.

Have the students prepare cucumbers in groups of three. Give each group different dressings and ideas on different ways of slicing them.

## Reflection

Have each group share and taste each other's cucumber creations. Discuss calories.

# Power of the Senses

## A High School Lesson for Art, Computers, and Rhetoric

## Focus Activity

Have the students bring in magazine ads that really appeal to them. The teacher can start to collect some ads also, and bring them in for later discussion. The only criteria is that the ad really "speaks" to them in some way. Discuss some of the appeal of the way the ad was put together.

## Activity

The following week, after several ads have been collected, the teacher should assign students into study groups of three. This will become their advertising study group.

The teacher will hold up some ads that are very appealing to the eye, and generate a brief discussion about what is so captivating about both the photos and the copy. Then the teacher will give each group of three students several ads to look at in their groups. The teacher will assign the roles of:

- timer

- recorder

- reporter.

The timer will give the group ten minutes for the task (a longer time frame may be needed if each group has more than three ads). The group's task is to discuss what is appealing about the ad. The recorder writes a few notes about each ad for the group reporter to report back to the entire class. The teams are also to discuss whether or not they would purchase that product. Primarily, they are to focus on what is specifically appealing and sensory about the ads they are viewing.

After the time is up, the reporter will share what their group discussed.

What will follow here is a mini-lecture on the power of advertising. The English teacher can handle the writing and composition portion, and the computer teacher and the art or photography teacher can share their visual knowledge. All of the teachers can generate "fat" questions that ask the students to analyze, judge, and evaluate. The teachers will conclude this input section with the question, "What affect does advertising have on them?"

The following day, or the same day if you have time, give each team computer time to print out a few appealing ads from the Internet. Have them go through the same discussion process to see what is appealing about that ad (one ad per group is fine for this activity). Briefly discuss how the Internet has influenced our lives. Now the teacher will pose this question to each group, "Using what you know about advertising, how would you create an influential and sensory-rich advertisement for one of your favorite healthy foods?" Make certain they get approval on their healthy food from the teacher before they proceed. If necessary, this would be a good time for the teacher to briefly discuss what foods are healthful. This checklist would be helpful to use.

## Checklist for a Healthful Food

Fresh from the ground (fresh fruits, veggies, nuts, seeds, sprouts)

Lean protein (skinless chicken, non-fried fish)

Free of preservatives

Free of food coloring

Unadulterated grains

Any combination thereof

Each team will have an entire class period to create this advertisement on the computer. The following day, the teams will try and "sell" their healthful food to the rest of the class.

The ads should be evaluated through class-generated rubrics and a team self-evaluation.

## Reflection

Have the students answer questions on a piece of paper to be collected by the teacher, such as:

What did you learn today?

What did you like about today's lesson?

What did you do well?

What concerns, if any, do you have about advertising and food?

# Chapter 2
## Malnutrition of the Brain

*"To my mind, one of the greatest offenses against a man is to deprive him of the normal supply of nourishment during infancy. It gives a bad start. He is shorn of his natural rights. The present abundance of nursing bottles and infants' foods in the drug stores is evidence of degeneration."*

*– Shall Our Children Be Sacrificed?*
*by Ephraim Cutter*

Of the three food groups mentioned in the introduction, the third group, junk food, may be the predominant fare for many children. Junk food, in fact, leads to malnutrition of the brain. If children are receiving most of their daily calories from overly-processed foods, they are crowding out room for the more nutrient-dense foods their brains need to function. Carol Simontacchi reports in her book, *The Crazy Makers: How the Food Industry Is Destroying Our Brains and Harming Our Children:*

"… adults don't eat any better than kids. According to national statistics and my client records gathered over years of nutritional consulting, it is not uncommon to see a seven-day food diary containing 21 meals with almost no vegetables, fruit, protein, or water…" (Simontacchi, 2000, p. 23).

The very hungry brain requires just the right amount of vitamins, minerals, amino acids, water and blood sugar flowing through it moment by moment to function optimally. If the amount of one of these nutrients drops, so does optimal brain functioning. This small yet busy organ only takes up about 3% of a grown person's body weight, yet it consumes 25–30% of its fuel in the form of blood sugar or glucose. Thus the brain is small, busy, fussy and incessantly hungry – constantly demanding fuel to do its job. One reason for the brain's continual "hunger" is that there is no room for nutrient storage in the brain. Saving up for a rainy day is out of the question in the cranial cavity. The brain relies solely on calories from food to do its work and has absolutely no reserves for periods of famine. That's why foods containing necessary nutrients are of great importance, as the brain does not rely on the generosity of the body's organs to share their limited stores of carbohydrates. The liver can release enough of its glucose stores to keep the brain chemicals balanced for only 24 hours. Muscles give up nothing to the blood. If we add calorie deprivation from poor diet, the brain has about as much patience as a hungry newborn baby. A lack of nutrients to the brain means an immediate cutback on the production of the chemical that supports the mind and keeps it peaceful (Pawlak, 2005). This chemical is called serotonin, and it plays a pivotal role in regulating moods. When serotonin levels are too low, depression, anxiety, hopelessness or rage is often commonplace. This is a recipe for failure. When you then add the inevitable level of stress to a hungry brain that is already barely limping along, this may be the straw that breaks the camel's back. The human brain does not take famine lightly.

> A lack of nutrients to the brain means an immediate cutback on the production of the chemical that supports the mind and keeps it peaceful (Pawlak, 2005).

Thiamine, which is Vitamin B-1, is a water-soluble, organic substance whose main task is to break down carbohydrates from food and convert them to glucose, the main brain fuel. Ironically, eating too many simple sugars (carbohydrates) depletes the body, and thus the brain, of this important vitamin. The result is a malnourished brain.

Water-soluble vitamins are not stored in the body and thus must be replenished daily. Foods high in thiamine include whole wheat, split peas, green peas, sunflower seeds, pork, brown rice, pecans, milk and most vegetables.

Even a mild thiamine deficiency can lead to lack of energy, moodiness, numbness in the legs, mild depression, loss of appetite, and a general feeling of apathy.

Another important vitamin for optimum brain functioning is Vitamin B-6, or pyridoxine. This vitamin aids in the synthesis of all monoamines, our natural mood enhancing neurotransmitters. For example, dopamine synthesis requires the amino acid tyrosine along with the cofactor vitamin B-6 and other nutrients. Vitamin B-6 also helps to convert tryptophan into serotonin.

A vitamin B-6 deficiency is the main culprit in a disease called pyroluria. Pyroluria is genetic defect of kryptopyrrole production. Kryptopyrroles, or pyrroles, are a worthless byproduct of hemoglobin synthesis. Most people have very few, if any, pyrroles circulating in their bodies. These pyrroles bind to aldehydes throughout the body, causing their excretion along with the pyrroles. Pyridoxine, or vitamin B-6, is an aldehyde, and thus removed from many sites to which it is vital, including the brain. The brain suffers a loss of B-6 in several ways. Vitamin B-6 is the co-enzyme (meaning it is absolutely essential) in more than 50 enzymatic brain reactions where amino groups are transformed. This vitamin is needed to achieve chemical balance in the nervous system. Without vitamin B-6, brain depletion of dopamine and serotonin occur, creating anxiety and depression. Without adequate serotonin, there will be erratic sleep and ongoing irritability.

Foods containing vitamin B-6 include kidney beans, sunflower seeds, broccoli, brussels sprouts, carrots, cauliflower, lentils, lima beans, peas, brown rice, salmon, spinach, tomatoes and tuna.

In the 1970s, Dr. Carl Pfeiffer confirmed the presence of what he called the "mauve factor" in the urine of normal individuals under stress or suffering from mental illness. He confirmed what others in the 1960s suspected: that a cluster of psychological and physical symptoms are identifiable in people whose urine turns mauve in color after certain laboratory tests. These people have a low tolerance for stress and a high level of inner tension and anxiety, which steadily worsens with age. They may also suffer from depression.

# Where Do Neurotransmitters Come From?

The breakdown of blood sugar in the brain to produce energy leads to the production of a series of chemical messenger substances called neurotransmitters. Neurotransmitters act like chemical intercoms in the nervous system – delivering messages from one portion of the body to another, including those that regulate mood, mind, memory and behavior. In fact, neurotransmitters are involved in everything we do. The only raw materials from which we can manufacture neurotransmitters is from the foods we eat. Thus, eating becomes much more important than just providing a moment of pleasure on our tongues and a full sensation in our bellies.

> Neurotransmitters are involved in everything we do.

## DID YOU KNOW?

The brain controls chemical releases from neurotransmitters in part through the proper production of energy from the breakdown of blood sugar in brain tissue. The only raw materials from which the brain can manufacture neurotransmitters are from the foods we eat.

# The Importance of Plant Foods for the Brain

The most recent research favors mother nature's best offerings, plant foods. If we consumed 11 servings of vegetables daily, we would be better off nutritionally than if we consumed 11 servings of white bread. Only about 8% of the population consumes the recommendations set by the National Cancer Institute of five servings of fruits and vegetables a day. And that's five combined servings of both fruits and vegetables. Some children rarely see a fresh vegetable in their daily diets.

# Phytochemicals in Plant Foods

In the 1980s, scientists discovered more exciting healthful components in plant foods other than the various fibers. These components are called phytochemicals, and they have revolutionized the status of plant foods to ones that are absolutely critical to good nutrition. "Phyto" comes from the Greek word meaning plant; thus the term phytochemical refers to natural plant-based chemicals that have been identified as active compounds in disease prevention. These plant components are not vitamins or minerals, but are in a class of their own, phytochemicals. They help regulate bodily functions and protect us from some diseases. Today there have been more than 10,000 different phytochemicals identified. They work to fine-tune the metabolic processes and help maintain health. Scientists are still discovering more about phytochemicals and their healthy properties. But one of the very most important properties of phytochemicals is that they seem to protect the brain.

# Beverage Brain Bombs

Americans have a love affair with soft drinks. They contain nothing that the body needs in terms of nutrients; in fact their ingredients are harmful. Colas contain coloring, sugar in abundance, and something called phosphoric acid. Phosphoric acid leaches calcium from the body. Diet soft drinks contain aspartame which has a harmful effect on the brain and body and does not feed the hungry brain.

> Diet soft drinks contain aspartame which has a harmful effect on the brain and body.

In 1983, the Centers for Disease Control (CDC) published results from a CDC study on consumer-based complaints associated with food products containing aspartame. Among them were insomnia and seizures. Gastrointestinal complaints were also reported, including abdominal pain, nausea and diarrhea. Irregular menses were reported in women.

Artificial sweeteners containing aspartame are sold under several brand names. One of the major problems with this sweetener is that it tends to remove chromium from the body. Chromium is a trace mineral important in the regulation of blood sugar in the body. Remember that blood sugar is the main fuel of the brain, and nothing should interfere with its production.

Aspartame is chemically synthesized. One of aspartame's components is methanol, which is wood alcohol. An excess of methanol can cause blindness and even death. Heat increases the rate of aspartame's conversion back to methanol. Because aspartame breaks down into methanol over time, it's important to keep any products containing aspartame cool. Also, do not store products containing aspartame for long periods of time.

Dr. Russell Blaylock in his book, *Excitotoxins: The Taste That Kills* (1997), labels aspartame an excitotoxin, which means it belongs in a group of excitatory amino acids that can cause the death of sensitive neurons.

One more reason to stay away from aspartame is that it triggers the appestat as though real food is entering the body. However, real food it is not. Thus, it stimulates the appetite, making a person hungry.

Aspartame is used as a sweetener in a large number of products, many of them consumed daily by children. Some of these products include yogurt, ice-cream, fruit drinks, cereals, soft drinks, gelatin desserts, vitamins, and medicines. Aspartame is also used in flavored coffee and many baked goods. This is not the liquid answer to weight loss or sugar reduction. Water is the preferred liquid nutrient. Diet soda has no food value; thus, it cannot feed the hungry brain.

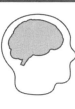

**BRAIN JOGGER**

Have the students anonymously write down what they ate for breakfast. Classify the results into the three food groups (Plant, Animal, Junk). As a class, discuss the results.

# MYTH: Milk is the Perfect Food

Is milk is the perfect food? Yes, but only if you are a baby cow. Humans are the only mammals on earth that drink the milk of another mammal, and the milk from the cow is not manufactured with our digestive tract in mind. (That could be because we are stealing milk from the calf.) This food is vastly overrated due in great part to the National

Dairy Council, which spends millions of dollars touting its products.

Milk contains 60% saturated fat. The fat globules in cows' milk are very large and difficult to digest for humans. Many individuals suffer from gastrointestinal problems such as gas bloating and diarrhea after consuming dairy

## DID YOU KNOW?

Cows' milk is one of the two or three most common food allergins in the American diet, both for children and adults.

products. Often, people develop allergies or sensitivities to milk.

In his book, *Dr. Braly's Food Allergy and Nutrition Revolution*, Dr. James Braly writes, "It is the major contributing factor to middle-ear infections (otitis media) in infants" (Braly, 1992, p. 294). Other symptoms associated with milk allergies include asthma, eczema, migraines, juvenile rheumatoid arthritis, chronic upper respiratory infections and congestion, bronchitis, pneumonia, bed-wetting, fatigue, hyperactivity, and even epilepsy in children who have allergy-related migraines.

A true milk allergy is a response to the casein in milk. However, the inability to digest milk may be explained by the fact that most people cannot digest lactose, a sugar found only in milk. Lactose intolerance means that an individual lacks the enzyme lactase necessary for the digestion of lactose. The lactase enzyme appears in the intestinal tract of infants during the last trimester of pregnancy, and peaks shortly after birth. Between 18 months and four years of age, however, most individuals throughout the world gradually lose the lactase activity in the small intestine, a clue that perhaps human beings are not meant to drink milk beyond early childhood. Some symptoms of lactose intolerance are gas, bloating, stomach cramps, diarrhea, constipation and indigestion.

Another problem with milk involves the homogenization process which, while extending milk's shelf life, also damages the fat in milk. Normal milk fat occurs in large globules usually digested intact in the intestinal tract. Homogenization breaks up these fat globules into extremely small droplets that are dispersed into the milk. Dr. Kurt Oster, chief of cardiology emeritus at Park City Hospital in Bridgeport, Connecticut, states:

"… much of the homogenized fat particles can bypass digestion and absorb directly into the bloodstream, carrying with them a destructive enzyme called xanthine oxidase (XO), that is protected by liposomes (membrane like packets). As it is carried through the bloodstream, XO can damage the arteries by attacking plasmalogen, an integral part of the art ery wall …" (in Gittleman, 1996).

Remember that there are arteries that lead directly to the brain.

For some of us, this perfect food called milk just leads to malnutrition of the brain. As early on as we can all remember, our parents, our teachers, and our grandparents all recited the same mantra: "Drink your milk." Milk is just about as American as apple pie and the flag. To disagree with any authority on the subject of milk is simply un-American. In fact, it is sacrilegious! But many people are allergic or sensitive to milk. It is certain that you know someone who is lactose intolerant. Or perhaps you know someone whose doctor said not to give cows' milk to their infant after the child had been weaned. That's because the milk they consumed during their childhood was different from the milk children consume today. Our grandparents drank milk that was delivered by a milk truck from the dairy farm. The milk came in bottles and the cream rose to the top of the bottle. It looked like a thick whipped cream on top, and that is exactly what it was. You shook the bottle to make the whole milk we know today. Milk, back then, was not homogenized.

The process of homogenization extends the shelf life of the milk. During this process, the fat in the milk is damaged. Homogenization breaks up the fat globules into extremely small droplets that are dispersed into the milk. Some of these fat particles can bypass the digestive system and become absorbed directly into the bloodstream. This is where the danger occurs, because also being absorbed into the bloodstream are particles of the destructive enzyme XO, which can damage arteries (Oster, in Gittleman, 1996). This fact alone should deter us from consuming so much milk. Yet we still repeat the mantra our parents chanted to us, "drink your milk."

The subject of milk is still a touchy one in schools because milk is subsidized by the government, and schools usually encourage milk consumption. For some children this is fine, but for others who suffer from allergies or sensitivities to dairy products, one small carton of milk can ruin their day. Let's face it, Americans have a love affair with all of the dairy products that come from cows' milk. We love cheese, sour cream, cream cheese, cottage cheese, frozen yogurt, ice-cream, whipped cream, milkshakes, and milk chocolate. These lusty high-fat foods from the udder of the cow have come to be adored by most Americans.

# Of Politics and Milk

Many of us were brought up thinking the National Dairy Council was a benevolent organization whose purpose was pure and wholesome. The name seems to imply an impartial group of individuals who come together to provide their wisdom and council. When they told us milk was "nature's most perfect food," we believed them. Most of us were told to drink a glass with every meal. This benign organization is organized to sell the American public as much milk as possible (Robbins, 1987).

The trade magazine, *Dairyman*, explains:

"It's important to understand the unique role the Dairy Council plays in promoting milk. The Dairy Council does no paid consumer advertising. That non-commercial status is important. As a highly respected education entity its programs give the dairy industry entry into areas difficult to penetrate with straight products promotion, especially the schools and medical-dental profession" (cited in Hausmen, 1981).

The National Dairy Council has had entry into schools for a very long time. The Basic Four Food Groups were created in 1956 by the United States Department of Agriculture (USDA). This was the beginning. In 1930 there were 12 food groups, and in 1944 it was narrowed to seven. Following World War II, heavy machinery and "favorable interest" financing became accessible to American farmers. As they plowed freshly-irrigated fields on brand-new tractors, large amounts of grains and soybeans were produced. To some degree the food habits cultivated by us, have been influenced by our nation's development (Klaper, 1987). This influence has caused a reverence toward this highly fat-saturated food, which happens to be one of the most common food to which people are allergic. Food allergies can mean brain allergies.

Speaking of which, it is time to take a quick tour through the hungry brain.

**BRAIN JOGGER**

Ask the students if anyone has a milk allergy, or is lactose intolerant (a sensitivity).

Tally the results.

Now ask how many students have a friend or relative who is lactose intolerant, or allergic to milk.

Ask the students if they are aware of any cows' milk substitutes.

# A Trip through the Brain

Just in the last decade, the concept of a "fixed brain" has been disregarded. New research is proving the nature of the brain to be ever-changing. The cells of this organ continually produce new dendrites and receptors, grow new synapses or communication junctions, and alter the essence of the neurotransmitter concoction that stimulates brain activity. Scientists are now taking an interest in how a person can influence the factors that control brain functioning through lifestyle changes including food and food supplements.

### DID YOU KNOW?

Years ago many scientists disbelieved their colleagues who thought food affected the brain.

Recent and not-so-recent research shows that nutrients, including glucose and fat, can have an almost immediate impact on brain cells and brain functioning, producing rapid changes in mood and behavior. In the early 1950s, pioneers in the field of nutrition and behavior were discredited as heretics. Some of these courageous pioneers were Abrams Hoffer, Humphrey Osmond, Carl Pfeiffer, Doris Rapp, Linus Pauling, Alan Cott, Bernard Rimland, Lendon Smith, William Crook and William Walsh. Today, their nutrition and brain connection findings are looked at seriously.

Brain metaphors abound. The soggy computer, the machine, the hardwire hardware. These all have been used to describe the brain at one time or another. But new brain research deems the computer metaphor unsatisfying. If the demands on your computer outstrips its capabilities, it becomes trash. It does not grow a few more chips. Its physical make-up is decreed forever by circumstances of its birth in some large computer factory. You can curse it, make it listen to music and give it nutrients, but it does not get any smarter. This is not true of your very own living brain.

The idea of brain as computer or machine is a vestige of yesterday's science. New investigations show it to be a growing, ever-changing complexity of cells. Jean Carper writes in her book, *The Miracle Brain*:

"The brain is a growing, changing organ, its capabilities and vitality dependent to a large degree on how you nourish and treat it. Thus, you can dramatically influence your brain's functioning and your own destiny. The long-neglected brain is now being exposed to intense biological scrutiny and the news is good for all of us" (Carper, 2000).

> "The long-neglected brain is now being exposed to intense biological scrutiny and the news is good for all of us" (Carper, 2000).

The busiest organ in the body is always working overtime. Even when we sleep, we dream. That's why the brain, our master controller of everything, needs proper care. Ten billion brain nerve cells process countless amounts of information each second. We are what we are because of our brain wiring, and what we eat or don't eat each day (Giuffre, 1999). To fully understand why certain foods empower while other foods disempower the brain, it helps to know a little about how the brain works.

The brain is subdivided into four major areas. They are, from top to bottom, the: (1) cerebral cortex; (2) midbrain; (3) brainstem; and (4) cerebellum.

# The Cerebral Cortex

The cerebral cortex, sometimes referred to as the cortex. This is the part that separates humans from all other mammals. Some scientists believe that the area in the front, appropriately named the frontal cortex, is where our complex and abstract thoughts occur. This is where problems are solved and reasoning takes place. It is said that the cortex houses the intellect, memory, language skills, and ability to understand symbols (Barrett, 1992). The frontal cortex acts as a bridge between the sensory and motor circuits of the rest of the cortex and the older, deeper structures of the limbic system, which regulate drive and emotions.

---

### DID YOU KNOW?

The cerebral cortex comprises about 85% of the brain's total mass and is divided into two halves, or hemispheres: the right hemisphere and the left hemisphere.

---

Each of these hemispheres contains different networks of cells that receive, store and retrieve information.

Behind the frontal cortex are the sensory and motor regions of the cortex, each divided up to correspond with specific areas on the opposite side of the body. Along the sides are two protruding horns called the temporal lobes. Here, much of the processing of sound and verbal information takes place.

■ □ ■ □ ■

In the back is the occipital cortex, where much of the processing of visual information occurs. The remaining parts along the side and above the temporal horns form the parietal cortex. The parietal cortex is thought to be where a lot of cross-connection between the different sensory structures take place. The parietal cortex or lobe is associated with touch and feeling received from the skin. This lobe senses hot and cold, hard and soft, and pain. It is also responsible for the sniffing and tasting sensations.

## The Midbrain

The midbrain is also called the limbic system. The primary parts of the limbic system are the hippocampus, the amygdala, the hypothalamus, the thalamus and the pituitary gland.

The hippocampus governs the storage of unemotional facts. As the brain's memory center, the hippocampus stores some short-term and a few long-term memories. It is the part of the brain that processes most "book learning" or semantic memory. In Alzheimer's patients, the hippocampus is among the first areas of the brain to be damaged. That is why most Alzheimer's patients lose their short-term memories before they lose their long-term memories. Most of the long-term memories are already stored in the neocortex (Khalsa, 1997).

Next to the hippocampus is the amygdala. According to some researchers, is the main processing area for emotional memories. Whereas the hippocampus is the regulator of the facts, the amygdala is the regulator of emotions. The memory of your first kiss was probably processed by the amygdala.

The thalamus monitors and sorts out messages from the senses so we don't get confused and move the wrong body part. It is about the size of a walnut, and assists in regulating our emotional life and physical safety. It is the main switching area of the sensory system.

The hypothalamus houses the emotions and regulates body temperature (without it we would be cold-blooded, like reptiles). It controls blood pressure and is the source of sexual feelings. It lets us know when we are hungry or thirsty. This organ is tiny, but important in controlling body temperature and organ functions.

The pituitary gland is connected to the hypothalamus. It controls the release of hormones that enable the body to produce energy out of the food we eat. The pituitary sends many hormones into the bloodstream to control the body's stress responses, sexual responses, menstrual cycles, and overall development and growth.

# The Brainstem: Involuntary Control Center

The brainstem is sometimes called the "hind brain" or the "lower brain." This is where the upper brain connects with the spinal cord. This area controls the autonomic nervous system, which is what directs the organs we don't voluntarily control, such as the heart, digestive tract, blood vessels, blood pressure, bladder and sexual organs. The brainstem is like the light switch of the cortex. It sends axons of nerve cells that comprise the stimulant amine neurotransmitters of norepinephrine, serotonin, dopamine, and histamine. These neurotransmitters are essential to the alert conscious state and when out of balance can result in depression, mood swings, aggressive behavior, attention problems, and narcolepsy (uncontrollably falling asleep) (Walsh, 1999).

Control areas for eye movement are also located in the brainstem. These are the switching areas for hearing and balance, as well as the motor and sensory connection areas for the face, nose and mouth. All of the spinal cord nerves to and from the cortex pass through here, along with those to and from the cerebellum.

# The Cerebellum: Voluntary Control Center

The cerebellum sits behind the brainstem and consists of a regular, repeating pattern of nerve cells. It coordinates or finetunes our automatic movement patterns, coordinating the muscles, posture, and motion. It is responsible for our being able to pick up a glass of water without spilling the water. When we run a race or use the computer keyboard or practise the piano, it's the cerebellum that shifts the muscles into automatic pilot. Activities such as playing a musical instrument, walking, running, riding a bicycle or picking up an object would be impossible without assistance from the cerebellum. And once we learn these activities they are performed automatically.

# Feeding the Brain

The brain is the busiest organ in the body; a chemical factory that never rests. Although comprising only 3% of total body weight, the brain uses about 30% of the body's fuel, called blood sugar in the form of glucose. Because the brain does not have any room for food storage, it will need a constant flow of vitamins, minerals, amino acids

> Although comprising only 3% of total body weight, the brain uses about 30% of the body's fuel, called blood sugar in the form of glucose.

and glucose in just the right amounts to feed it for proper functioning. If one of these nutrients is in short supply, the brain will be in sub-optimal working condition. The way the brain receives these nutrients is from the foods we eat.

# When Brain Cells Talk to One Another

As a means of controlling the process of providing fuel to the brain, it's important to know that brain cells talk to each other by way of neurotransmitters. You have probably heard of two of them, serotonin and dopamine. In the brain, small chunks of information are passed as messages both within the brain cell by means of electrical impulses and between cells by chemical transfer. This chemical transfer is accomplished via the dopamine and norepinephrine transmitters, the brain's alertness neurotransmitters; gamma amino butyric acid (GABA), its natural sedative neurotransmitter; and serotonin, the brain's natural mood stabilizer and sleep promoter. Every function imaginable, from reading a book to kissing a loved one, involves neurotransmitters.

> Every function imaginable, from reading a book to kissing a loved one, involves neurotransmitters.

Because neurotransmitters play this constant and critical role in the work of the brain, they need a continuous source of nutrients for building and sending messages. The only raw materials available to create these neurotransmitters are through the foods we eat.

## DID YOU KNOW?

The only raw materials from which we manufacture neurotransmitters are from the foods we eat.

Feeding the brain before a day of learning is just as important as arriving to school prepared with homework. What are these food fuels that are needed by the brain and where do they come from? Fruits provide vitamins; vegetables and whole grains are sources for needed minerals; and protein foods supply the amino acids and some of the fatty acids that are essential for the brain. Water is another nutrient that keeps everything working properly.

# Vitamins

Thiamine, vitamin B-1, is a water-soluble vitamin with
the task of breaking down carbohydrates from food and
converting them into glucose, the sugar that provides fuel
needed to run the brain.

About 100 years ago, widespread thiamine (vitamin
B-1) deficiency followed the introduction of polished rice,
which is rice with its outer seed coats of bran removed.
Bran contains most all of the important nutrients, so there is
very little left of any nutritional value after bran's removal.
Thiamine deficiency was prevalent where rice is a staple,
for example, in eastern Asia, South America, and the Pacific
islands. The symptoms of thiamine deficiency are numbness,
respiratory and cardiac disorders, and memory loss. At that
time, severe memory failure was called "beri beri amnesia"
(Cherkin, in Essman 1987).

One study on thiamine deficiency occurred after the
surrender of 32,000 British troops in Singapore in 1942.
The abrupt change from normal British army rations to a
diet of polished rice where the outer bran was removed
was followed within six weeks by numerous symptoms
of thiamine deficiency. The troops' mind-related changes
started with anxiety and continued with memory loss and
disorientation. The principal researchers, de Wardener and
Lennox (1947), concluded that thiamine deficiency was the
main factor in the observed symptoms. When thiamine was
administered, patients' symptoms were reversed, rapidly
and consistently.

Larson (1997) reports that alcohol blocks thiamine
absorption, causing neurological symptoms including
memory loss, nervousness, headaches and poor
concentration. This alcohol-induced thiamine deficiency is
the cause of Wernicke-Korsakoff syndrome, the irreversible
brain deterioration that can occur in the later stages of
alcoholism.

■ □ ■ □ ■

Another vitamin important for optimum brain functioning is vitamin B-6 or pyridoxine. Pyridoxine aids in the syntheses of all monoamines. Monoamines are a class of neurotransmitters that include serotonin, dopamine, and norepinephrine. These are our natural mood-enhancing neurotransmitters. These important brain chemicals cannot be manufactured properly in the brain without the presence of vitamin B-6 (Ross, 1999). Food sources of vitamin B-6 include chicken, beef liver and, to a lesser extent, fortified oatmeal and other cuts of beef.

> Food sources of vitamin B-6 include chicken, beef liver and, to a lesser extent, fortified oatmeal and other cuts of beef.

# Minerals, Moods, and More

It has been known since 1939 that vitamins control the body's appropriation of minerals, but, lacking minerals, vitamins are useless. There are two groups of minerals, macro and trace. Macro minerals that are needed in larger amounts include calcium, magnesium, sodium, potassium, and phosphorus. Trace minerals, needed in lesser amounts but of no less importance to the brain, include zinc, boron, iron chromium, selenium, and iodine. For example, boron is needed for calcium uptake; iodine helps metabolize excess fat and is needed for a healthy thyroid gland; and chromium is involved in the metabolism of glucose.

> Minerals are a "spark plug" to the brain.

There are 22 known minerals that are vital to health. As the body does not manufacture minerals, it must get them from foods. Minerals are found in a wide variety of foods called vegetables and legumes (beans); and leafy greens, such as kale, Swiss chard, collard greens and mustard greens. Ocean fish, sea vegetables, almonds, sunflowers and sesame seeds are also high in minerals. Some of these are foods that many kids have not learned to eat. There is a growing concern that many children are low in nutrients, including the minerals calcium, iron, and zinc (Sinatra, 1996).

Brain function depends on minerals. Minerals activate neural communication, regulate brain metabolism, and protect the brain from toxic metal contamination. Minerals are also catalysts for a number of biological functions, especially growth and healing. Minerals are a "spark plug" to the brain.

# Zinc

Zinc is often called the intelligence mineral because it is involved in so many brain functions. Not only is it required for mental development, zinc is also needed for healthy reproductive organs, particularly the prostate gland, for protein syntheses and collagen formation. Zinc is also needed to assist in blood sugar control, which is crucial to mood, memory and behavior. A zinc deficiency during pregnancy may cause birth defects (Pfeiffer, 1987).

Found in abundance in brain tissue, zinc is one of the most important trace minerals when it comes to the brain's functioning. This trace mineral is a component of more than 80 human enzymes. Some researchers postulate that zinc is a neurotransmitter. Zinc deficiency has been recognized as a factor in several physiological disorders. Among them are: slow wound healing; psoriasis; acne; eczema; growth retardation; delayed sexual maturation; poor immune functioning; irritability; poor stress control; premenstrual syndrome (female); attention deficit disorder; hyperactivity; white spots on the fingernails; easily sunburnt skin; and hypogeusia, which is poor taste acuity. It is clear that humans cannot function without zinc. New research has shown zinc to be far more important than we previously believed.

Doctors Walsh, Isaacson, Norman, Usman, Pfeiffer and others studied the effects and reasons for zinc deficiencies (Walsh, 2006). Many persons are born with a metal metabolism disorder that results in a deficiency of zinc regardless of diet. Zinc deficiency often results in elevated levels of copper in the blood because of the dynamic competition of these two trace minerals in the body. Elevated copper has been associated with attention deficit disorder, hyperactivity, depression, and schizophrenia (Walsh, 2006). In most cases, low levels of zinc appear to involve a malfunction of the metal-binding protein, metallothionein.

The job of the metallothionein protein is to take in metals, tell them where to go in the body, and discard the excess metals that are not necessary or toxic in nature. When this process is impaired, problems can occur. A person may store excess copper, thus depleting the very important zinc. This may result in mood swings, irritability, and the health impairments mentioned previously. Additionally, an imbalance of the appropriate copper/zinc ratio could also cause extreme sensitivities to such things as food dyes because, with a metallothionein protein malfunctioning, the body cannot get rid of excess chemical toxins  (Walsh et al. 1994).

> Food sources for zinc include oysters, ginger-root, round steak, lamb, pecans, peas, shrimp, parsley and potatoes.

Along with the B vitamins, zinc is particularly important in helping the brain manufacture neurotransmitters out of the amino acids from proteins. Chronic alcohol consumption and high sugar intake often force the body to excrete zinc, causing a shortage of it (Larson, 1997).

Food sources for zinc include oysters, ginger-root, round steak, lamb, pecans, peas, shrimp, parsley and potatoes. You can see how easy it is for our children to fall short of zinc considering they would not frequently consume these foods.

# Chromium

Chromium, a trace mineral, is also very important for the child and adult's hungry brain. It works with insulin in the metabolism of sugar and makes the insulin work more efficiently, thereby helping to maintain normal blood glucose levels. This is a blessing for individuals with glucose regulation problems. Chromium helps to stabilize the glucose curve by raising brain levels of glucose that are too high, and lowering brain levels of glucose that are too low.

> Good food sources of chromium include brewer's yeast, broccoli, ham, turkey, grape juice, grapefruit and shellfish.

Eating too many empty calorie, sugary foods depletes the chromium level in the body. Good food sources of chromium include brewer's yeast, broccoli, ham, turkey, grape juice, grapefruit and shellfish.

# Magnesium

As minerals go, magnesium has hardly achieved superstar status; however, it is very much a superstar in terms of the work it performs. Few people ponder whether or not they are receiving enough magnesium daily. Yet, each day the busy brain uses magnesium to function optimally.

Magnesium plays an important role in keeping brain cells alive. It minimizes the negative effects of reduced blood flow and increases the ability of neurons to receive nutrients by increasing cell membrane fluidity. It is also important for converting blood sugar into energy, and necessary for effective nerve and muscle functioning.

Magnesium is used in more than 300 enzymes, many of which are brain enzymes (Simontacchi, 2000). Building strong bones, regulating body temperature, releasing energy from muscles, and manufacturing proteins are more of the important functions of the body that need magnesium's help. Magnesium also prevents calcium build-up, which is a phenomenon that frequently kills brain cells. Magnesium helps produce a calming effect on the brain.

Food sources of magnesium include raw nuts and seeds, legumes, whole grains, dark green leafy vegetables, bananas, dried apricots, dry mustard, curry powder and cocoa.

Low levels of magnesium have been linked to aggressive behavior, alcoholism, anxiety, attention deficit disorder, over-excitability, PMS, dementia, depression, fatigue, autism, insomnia, learning disabilities and schizophrenia (Werbach, 2000).

Food sources of magnesium include raw nuts and seeds, legumes, whole grains, dark green leafy vegetables, bananas, dried apricots, dry mustard, curry powder and cocoa.

## More on Plant Foods

More than $20 million has been spent in the past several years on research to evaluate the anticancer potential of plant foods (Pawlak, 1999). Some of the foods and herbs with the highest anti-cancer activity were found to be garlic, soybeans, ginger, licorice and the umbelliferous vegetables, which include carrots, celery, cilantro, parsley and parsnips. Some foods and spices with a moderate to high level of cancer-protective activity are onions, flax, citrus, turmeric, cruciferous vegetables (including broccoli, brussels sprouts, cabbage and cauliflower), solanaceous vegetables (including tomatoes, eggplant and peppers), brown rice, whole wheat and barley. Researchers are still discovering new phytochemicals in plant foods to this day.

Devouring fruits and vegetables may slash your chances of heart attacks and strokes, even if you have already suffered one. Vegetarians have the lowest rate of heart disease (Carper, 2000). Women who ate one additional large carrot or half a cup of sweet potatoes or other foods rich in beta carotene each day slashed their risk of heart attack by 22% and stroke by 40 to 70%, according to Harvard research. Beta carotene is a carotenoid that comes from a red, orange or yellow coloring in plant food. Carotenoids are fat soluble antioxidants, and infiltrate cell membranes and other fatty structures in the same way as vitamin E (Carper, 2000).

In a Harvard study tracking more than 90,000 female nurses, those eating the most beta carotene had a 22% lower risk of heart disease than women getting less than 3,800 IU daily. The high-beta carotene eaters' risks of stroke were an even more impressive 37% lower.

> Devouring fruits and vegetables may slash your chances of heart attacks and strokes, even if you have already suffered one.

Beta carotene may also lengthen the human lifespan. Men who ate six milligrams of beta carotene daily (one carrot) for more than 25 years had a 28% lower risk of death (from any cause) compared with men eating the least beta carotene, reported University of Texas researchers.

Researchers have identified a host of active substances in fruits and vegetables that help protect against disease. Here is a partial list:

| Fruit or Vegetable | Disease Protection |
| --- | --- |
| Glucarates in citrus fruits, grains and tomatoes | Improve detoxification |
| Allyl sulfides in garlic and onions | Antioxidants, detoxification |
| Lignans in flax and soybeans | Normalize metabolism of estrogen and testosterone |
| Isoflavones in soybeans | Normalize activity of estrogen |
| Saponins in legumes | Anti-cancer agents |
| Ellagic acid in grapes, strawberries, raspberries and nuts | Anti-cancer agents |
| Indoles, isothiocyanates and hydroxybutene in cruciferous vegetables | Improve detoxification of carcinogens |
| Bioflavonoids, carotenoids and terpenoids in various other plant foods | Modify inflammation and immunity |
| Phytates in whole grains and legumes such as soy | Anti-cancer agents |
| P-Coumaric Acid and Chlorogenic Acid | Anti-cancer agents |
| Chlorophyll | Medical therapy for anemia |
| Soluble fiber called pectin | Drives down cholesterol |

These phytochemicals found in plant foods have also been found to protect the brain from ageing.

## DID YOU KNOW?

Corn is not a vegetable; it's a grain.

A tomato is a fruit.

The only fruit that has seeds on the outside of it is the strawberry.

## BRAIN JOGGER

Ask the students what malnutrition is.

Now ask them if they know what malnutrition of the brain is.

Have them draw a visual representation of what malnutrition of the brain means to them.

# BRAIN FOOD LESSONS

## Learning about Plant Foods

### An Elementary Lesson

## Focus Activity

Read the book *Tops and Bottoms* (Stevens, 1995 as an introduction.

Summary: Clever but poor Hare tricks rich but lazy Bear by offering to split the shared crop by "tops and bottoms". When Bear chooses top, Hare plants root vegetables such as carrots, leaving Bear nothing but worthless stalks and leaves. When Bear chooses bottoms, Hare plants corn leaving Bear nothing but empty stalks and roots.

The teacher will lead a discussion of the plant parts eaten in the story.

The teacher can talk about common, and not so common, varieties of plant leaves, stems, and roots that are use as food sources. Bring in a sunflower, (seeds) sweet potato (root), and so on.

The students will draw and label the leaf, stem and root of a plant food that they like. The students can color the picture.

## Activity

In groups of three assign the roles of:

- cutter

- tape or glue person

- arranger.

Give each group of three students, magazine pictures of plant foods, one pair of scissors, one piece of paper, and some glue or tape. Each group will have 15 minutes to create a collage of different plant foods and to create a name for the collage. During the collage making, one person cuts, another person arranges the picture on the page, and another person glues.

Have a checklist of criteria that you create as a class. For example, you might require several different-colored plant foods, for instance green, red, orange, purple. You may also require that the collage contain a pretty border, and that there be no negative space.

After the collage is complete arrange for each group to explore the Internet. Have the students visit 'Eat 5 a Day for Better Health' at www.healthyfood.org/sub/kids.html. This is from Yahooligans, and includes recipes and menu planning. After visiting the website, each team will write a story titled "The Meal that came from 'Plant It' Earth". The story is to be about an all plant meal, that people of the community thought was so weird, that it came from another planet. Give the groups as much time as you think they will need to complete the task. Share the stories, and post them around the room. Next day, have the groups assemble again, this time to write a persuasive paragraph to convince the community from their story to eat more plant foods.

As a culminating activity, have each group plan a plant food snack and have a "I came from Plant It Earth' party. Check records for possible food allergies and sensitivities.

## Reflection

Have the students reflect in their nutrition journals about a new plant food they might have tried during the "Plant It" activity.

# Out of the (Cereal) Box

## A Middle School Lesson

## Focus Activity

Ask the students to individually write down what they think a good breakfast is (give them two minutes). Now, have them share their list with a partner. Also, have them share what they ate for breakfast.

## Activity

Place students in groups of four and assign the following roles:

- timer
- materials manager
- recorder
- reporter.

The materials manager will gather the necessary materials: several colored markers, a large piece of newsprint and a couple of pieces of tape. The timer will give the groups five minute for this task. The task are for the recorded to write down on the large piece of paper what the group thinks makes a healthful breakfast. All group members must sign the paper. The material manager will tape the paper on the wall where the teacher has specified, and the reporter proceeds to report to the class the group's ideas.

As a class, the teacher leads the whole group into a discussion of what foods are commonly appearing on the posters. The teacher will then ask some questions of the class.

"Why do you think breakfast is important?"

"Who ate something out of the ordinary for breakfast this morning?"

See if anyone ate something that would be considered a dinner food, rather than a breakfast food.

See if anyone ate anything with protein in it. The teacher will than ask another question, "Does anyone know what people in other countries eat for breakfast?" Build a discussion around that question. In Japan, fish soup might be on the breakfast menu. In Israel, breakfast is the largest meal of the day, and it always includes a protein. In Mexico, eggs or beans might be wrapped in a tortilla. Now, have the students compare the foods they listed to the foods children in other countries might eat for breakfast.

## About Breakfast

A healthful breakfast begins with protein. Proteins are foods with a dense concentration of amino acids. Amino acids are the building blocks of proteins, just as bricks, mortar and other materials are the building blocks (parts) of the buildings in which you live. Foods high in protein are critical for breakfast because protein produce certain brain chemicals that make the brain alert and ready to learn. The names of these brain chemicals are dopamine and norepinephrine. They are called neurotransmitters. Neurotransmitters are involved in everything we do.

Eating protein in the morning is important for feeling good for the rest of the day. Without enough protein in the morning, the brain gets tired. It "poops out" for the rest of the day.

Skipping breakfast slows down the metabolism and induces food cravings later in the day. Another advantage of eating a healthful breakfast is that calorie burning is heightened by eating at least 20 or more grams of protein food (20 grams is about the size of an adult fist).

After the discussion and mini-lecture, the students can continue in the groups of four with the same job roles. Have the material manager gather one more piece of large newsprint. Divide the paper into quarters. Each group member will have their own quarter of the paper with which to work. The timer will give the groups 15 minutes for the task. The task is to have each student take their own piece of the quartered paper and draw and write what they now think is a healthful breakfast, and what they might personally do to change their own breakfast habits. This must be done by each individual in the group. This too can be drawn on the piece of the paper that each member is assigned to.

After the 15 minutes, have each group report their new breakfast findings. The groups will report as a foursome, but each individual will speak about their portion of the poster.

## Reflection

In their journals, have them reflect on changes they think they can make. Encourage them to be specific. Exactly what will they do? What can they do? What are they willing to do? Discuss.

# First Up

## A High School Lesson on Breakfast

## Focus Activity

Have the students write down on a piece of paper what they ate for breakfast that morning. If they did not eat anything at all, they are to write the word "nothing" on the paper. Have them stand up when they have completed the task. Now, without talking, instruct them to form a line in silence, rank-ordering themselves from healthful breakfast to non-healthful breakfast. The teacher will instruct the students as to where the healthful line begins. When the non-verbal communication has ceased, and the line is formed, the teacher then asks each person to show the class what they wrote on their paper and tell the class what they ate for breakfast. The line may or may not be "nutritionally accurate," but that's okay. While the students are standing, place them in groups of two, trying to put a non-breakfast-eater with one or two healthful breakfast-eaters. In other words, do not put three nothing for breakfast students in the same group.

## Activity

Have each group member read the passage titled: "About Breakfast".

## Reflection

Have the students form pairs and talk to their partner about what emotional reaction they had (if any) while reading the article. What went through their heads. What questions came up for them?

# Chapter 3
## Not All Fats Are Bad

*Eat, drink, and be sick, both physically and mentally.*

*– Theron, G. Randolph*

One of the most little-known facts about the human brain is that more than 60% of its structure is fat. Perhaps this is where the term "fat-head" originated! The hungry brain, however, is particular about the kind of fat it prefers. The nerves that allow us to jump, walk, talk, think, draw a picture or play the trombone all depend on just the right fats. Not any old fat will do.

As mentioned, the brain is dependent upon raw materials from the diet. Therefore, you could say, our brains are made from what we eat. Though able to manufacture some of what it needs, the brain is surprisingly dependent upon what its owner eats for breakfast, lunch, dinner and snacks. The right fats are important and, if not supplied, brain structure is altered (Schmidt, 1997).

> One of the most little-known facts about the human brain is that more than 60% of its structure is fat.

This is definitely a problem for school-aged children in the United States who consume nearly 40% of their calories from fat. However, this glut of fat has not translated into something beneficial for the busy brain – quite the reverse. The good fats are missing! Many Americans have switched to food containing animal fats and warm-weather vegetable oil as well as processed foods. But the brain is actually more in need of Omega-3 fatty foods such as cold-water fish, walnuts, greens, and flax seed oil.

> The good fats are missing!

■ □ ■ □ ■

In order to satisfy its vast demand for energy-supported products such as its blood supply, oxygen and nutrients, the brain commands about 20% of the heart's output. Memorizing a phone number, hitting a softball or finding the right birthday card for a friend all require blood flow to the brain. Mood, emotions, learning and behavior are also dependent upon blood flow to the brain, and so any restriction in the supply of blood weakens brain function; for this, there is no exception (Schmidt, 1997). Once again, therefore, diet is critical!

Scientists are beginning to learn that dietary factors may cause the blood vessels to begin narrowing early on in life. When doctors studied the blood vessels of children ranging from age one to fifteen, they discovered that the vessels already showed evidence of narrowing. Narrowed blood vessels were found even in the youngest children studied (Pesonen et al., 1991).

When these arteries were further analyzed for fatty acid composition, two striking findings stood out: the blood vessels were too low in Omega-3 fatty acids (EPA) and too high in Omega-6 fatty acids (linoleic acid). Another similar study of children aged three to eighteen found the same results.

What are the implications of these findings on school-aged children? From very early on in life, dietary fats have a profound effect on the vessels that supply vital oxygen and nutrients to the brain. Many children often consume an unbalanced diet in fats critical to maintaining the brain's healthy blood supply. This causes blood vessels early in life to begin narrowing, which will influence brain function throughout one's life (Schmidt, 1997).

## BRAIN JOGGER

Brainstorm a list of fish the children in your class have eaten.

Graph the names of the fish and the frequency consumed.

Count how many children have eaten something green in the past two weeks.

Have students create recipes using almonds.

In pairs, have the children name as many green vegetables as they can in one minute.
One person can write while the other names them.
Reverse roles. Count.

Like so many of us, you are probably shocked by the idea that fat can be a good component in your diet. The anti-fat movement has been very successful, though misguided, since the 1970s when Nathan Pritikin created the now famous Pritikin diet. Very low in fat, this diet hit the headlines and became extremely popular. What didn't make it into print was important information from the Pritikin Institute's own former head nutritionist, Ann Louise Gittleman. In her book *Beyond Pritikin*, Gittleman reported that Pritikin clients who went on very low fat (10%) diets for more than three months developed new health problems and regained unneeded weight. A big part of their new problems had to do with the loss of healthy fats along with unhealthy ones (Gittleman, 1996).

# The Brain and Fat

It may be somewhat surprising to many of us that the fibers woven to make up the tapestry of the brain are composed primarily of fat – but what kind?

In saturated fats, the carbons in the chain are completely "saturated" with all the hydrogen they can carry. The lamp neck completely covered with golf balls is an image used frequently to describe how this takes place. Saturated fats form relatively straight chains that bunch closely together. The result is dense, solid fat, like the white fat in beef and lamb that does not melt at room temperature.

> The fibers woven to make up the tapestry of the brain are composed primarily of fat.

In unsaturated fats, the carbons carry less hydrogen – the lamp neck has some space on it that is not covered in golf balls. Unsaturated fats are either monounsaturated or polyunsaturated.

As with carbohydrates, fats are sources of energy. The body needs fuel to function and fats are the most concentrated sources of food energy. Each gram of fat provides nine calories compared with only four calories a gram from carbohydrates.

After the body uses the fat we eat for energy, excess fat does not simply disappear. It is used by many different types of tissue, but the largest amount, by far, goes to the body's adipose, or fat, cells. These fat deposits not only store energy but also help to insulate the body and support and protect various organs. Fats also help us absorb the fat-soluble vitamins A, D, E, and K by serving as carrier for them in the intestines. The fact is, human beings need plenty of good fat in their diets and on their bodies for the production of all hormones and to protect their internal organs, insulate them from cold, make hair and skin lustrous, maintain mental stability and concentration, avoid carbohydrate cravings, and keep the bowels regular. Without enough body fat, women may also experience fertility problems.

# Essential and Nonessential Fats

There are two major types of essential fats and a third nonessential. The first two are Omega-3 oils from flax and fish, and Omega-6 oils from plant sources such as natural vegetable oils and borage and evening primrose oils. The third nonessential fat needs mentioning – it is called Omega-9 and is found in olive oil, almonds and avocados. Many scientists believe that Omega-9 fats are inappropriately labeled as nonessential. Their talents have been underutilized, like a second-string team.

For many years, eating a low fat diet was the popular strategy for just about everything, from losing weight to preventing certain cancers. These popular diets banned all fat and touted fat as the enemy. Many of these low fat or no fat food plans didn't acknowledge the beneficial value of any fat in the diet. These weight-loss efforts were misguided in that fat is a nutrient – in fact, a macro-nutrient. This means we need some fat – some good fat – every day.

In a 1978 study published in the British medical journal, *Lancet*, Drs. Bang and Dyerberg investigated the diet of native Greenland Eskimos. They reported that, despite an extremely high fat diet, the native people of Greenland had a very low incidence of coronary heart disease, diabetes, and cancer. As early as 1855 the connection between the Eskimos' diet of fish and their low incidence of heart disease was suspected. These early population studies were revisited after the Bang and Dyerberg study (Bang & Dyerberg 1978).

It was reported that the diet of the Greenland Eskimos contained more than 70% of its calorie content in fat, and yet they are free of killer degenerative illness such as heart disease. The key to the Eskimos' excellent health is the kind of fat they eat. They get their fat from marine life (seal, whale, walrus) and fatty cold-water fish that make up the bulk of their diet. These marine foods are high in two important fats from the Omega-3 fatty acid family called eicosapentaenoic acid, or EPA, and docosahexaenoic acid, or DHA. These two fatty acids have been shown to protect the heart and feed the brain (Gittleman 1996). EPA and DHA also assist in maintaining neuronal connections. If the body does not receive enough of these good fats, it is difficult for the brain to trigger endorphins, the feel-good neurotransmitters.

> Another important fat is called evening primrose oil.

Another important fat is called evening primrose oil which contains substantial amounts of an Omega-6 fatty acid called GLA, or gamma linolenic acid. In the early 1980s, Dr. David Horrobin began publishing research on GLA showing that it helped cardiovascular problems, weight loss, inflammation, alcoholism, disorders of the immune system, premenstrual syndrome, and skin, hair, and nail conditions (Horrobin, in Gittleman, 1996).

> Those who eat foods with monounsaturates enjoy better odds against cancer over their lifetimes.

Let's look at the Omega-9 fats, also known as monounsaturated. These have been quite the celebrity as they are popular in various regional diets, especially those of the Mediterranean countries. In the 1990s, the Mediterranean diet was looked at for its health effects. What do the people of this region eat? Lots of fruits and vegetables (much more than in the United States) – tomatoes, garlic and olive oil, loaded with the Omega-9 nonessential fatty acid. As Laura Pawlak reports in her book, *A Perfect 10: Phyto "New-trients" Against Cancers: A Practical Guide for the Breast, Prostate, Colon, Lung (1999)*, those who eat foods with monounsaturates enjoy better odds against cancer over their lifetimes. In an Italian study, researcher Anthony Capurso, M.D., of the University of Bari, found that among a group of 278 elderly southern Italians, those who consumed the most olive oil cut their odds of memory loss by one-third, their average amount being about three tablespoons per day (in Carper, 2001). Italians use olive oil extensively in cooking. Researchers suggest olive oil and fish oil help maintain the "structural integrity of neuronal membranes" and contain antioxidants that combat brain-cell-destroying free radicals.

> Researchers suggest olive oil and fish oil help maintain the "structural integrity of neuronal membranes".

Extra virgin olive oil is produced by crushing olives between stone or steel rollers. This process is the best way to preserve the integrity of the fatty acids and natural preservatives in this nutritious substance. If olive oil is packaged in an opaque container, it will retain both its freshness and its precious store of antioxidants for many months (Fallon, 1995).

Nature offers still another monounsaturate: the avocado fruit. Often perceived as a vegetable, the avocado is a delicious source of monounsaturated fat. Bring one to school one day for the students to taste.

# The Importance of Fats for the Brain

In her book *Your Miracle Brain*, Jean Carper writes:

"… Failure to eat enough Omega-3 fat is scientifically linked to an array of modern mental disorders and problems: depression, poor memory, low intelligence, learning disabilities, dyslexia, attention deficit disorder, schizophrenia, senility, Alzheimer's Disease, degenerative neurological diseases, multiple sclerosis, alcoholism, poor vision, irritability, hostility, inattention, lack of concentration, aggression, violence and suicide …" (Carper, 2001, p. 68).

■ □ ■ □ ■

Remembering that the brain is the busiest organ in the body, it therefore needs a continual supply of nutrients flowing through it moment by moment to maintain its abundant activity. Fat is one of those nutrients! Fats of the right type have a positive effect on brain functioning, while the wrong type of fat can have a deleterious effect on the brain.

As with olive oil, several studies have been conducted to examine the benefits of fish oil in the diet. Omega-3 is the main oil found in the ocean fish from which the fish oils are extracted. It's definitely one of the good fats. An abundant supply of fish oil can help defeat free radicals that destroy brain cells, reduce immune responses that trigger cell-damaging inflammation, change the behavior of neurotransmitters, and modify the basic physical structures of brain cells themselves (Carper, 2001).

# Fats and Cell Membranes

Each brain cell is protected by a membrane that keeps out unwanted intruders and controls the cell's internal workings through signaling mechanisms called receptors. Receptors are imbedded in the brain cell membrane. The membranes consist of two layers of fatty molecules. The membranes' flexibility depends on the fat's consistency. If the fat is hardened like the lard in the middle of a cupcake, the membrane is stiff and rigid; but if the fat is more fluid and oily, like fish oil, the membrane is pliable and soft.

Pliability of cell membranes is important for brain cell communication. Dr. Joseph Hibbeln from the National Institutes of Health (NIH) writes that it is especially true in the synapses of brain cells – the junctions where nerve cells converge to pass their messages along. According to Dr. Hibbeln, the more transmission centers, or synapses, on brain cells, the smoother the communication between them, and the better the brain functions (Hibbeln, in Carper,

2001). Fish oil, or more precisely the part called DHA (docosahexaenoic acid), is the material needed for building the synaptic communication centers. It's no fish tale that fish fat is definitely good fat!

# Fats to Avoid for Brain Health

As you amble through the grocery aisle, the words "fat free" and "low fat" often jump out at you from the wide array of packaged foods there. Many of us conclude that perhaps all fats are bad for us. And that's true in that too much of anything can be bad. However, a completely fat free diet is not healthy for the hungry brain. The brain's major structures need a number of fats to perform.

Plants and animals can make fats using building blocks known as fatty acids. Fatty acids that humans manufacture are called nonessential fatty acids because we do not

> A completely fat free diet is not healthy for the hungry brain.

need a food supply to make them. However, there are certain fatty acids that humans cannot manufacture, and they are essential to brain health. These are called essential fatty acids, and humans must obtain them from the foods they eat (Rudin and Felix, 1996). As the normal brain is more than 60% fat, essential fatty acids help the brain to function.

In fact, not just brain cells but every cell in the body depends on essential fatty acids for normal functioning.

The cell is a tiny yet powerful factory, taking in raw materials from its surrounding fluid and sending out various chemicals. The cells' outer surface (membrane) screens everything going in and coming out. The membrane depends on essential fatty acids to remain fluid and flexible. Without them, the membrane becomes stiff and unable to do its job.

■ □ ■ □ ■

# Phony Fats

The hungry brain needs a certain amount of saturated fat, polyunsaturated fat, cholesterol, and a number of other fats (Schmidt, 1997) for its cells to function. Hydrogenated fats and partially hydrogenated fats synthesized from natural fats are not among them. These fats are to be avoided. Unfortunately, these fats are found in many of the packaged foods purchased today, including many margarines.

How do you get liquid corn oil, from which the margarine is made, solid at room temperature? It must undergo a process called "hydrogenation". This is where margarine-making becomes hazardous to your health. The process of hydrogenation changes the chemical structure of the fat. Corn oil, a naturally unsaturated fatty acid, is converted by hydrogenation into an unnatural, saturated fat. Corn oil is converted from its cis form, which is natural, into an unnatural and unhealthy trans form of fat. Trans fats not only raise cholesterol levels faster than saturated fats, they also weaken the cell membranes that make up the body's immune system. These trans fats clog arteries to the heart and brain.

> These trans fats clog arteries to the heart and brain.

The packaging of margarine is deceiving for that reason. The food package label may state the product contains no cholesterol, and that is entirely true. What the food package label fails to tell you is that the hydrogenated oil, or the partially hydrogenated oil, is a trans fat that will raise your cholesterol level once you ingest it. This is more damaging to your heart than the cholesterol itself. So, yes, while the food itself does not contain cholesterol, the type of fat in the food will raise cholesterol in the body, clogging arteries to the heart, brain and legs.

The purpose of the hydrogenation process is to give the fat a longer shelf life and raise its melting point.

Hydrogenated fats are great for baking, and because of their durability are very economical for large-scale institution food. But, while hydrogenation adds to cooking convenience, it does so at the expense of the public's health.

Research by Dr. Fred Kummerow in 1974 confirmed the atherosclerotic effects of margarine made from trans fats on test animals. Twenty years later, a study conducted by Harvard researchers Walter Willett and Alberto Ascgerio found that the trans fats in margarine and in partially hydrogenated oils double the risk of heart attacks by lowering HDL, the good cholesterol, and raising LDL, the bad.

In 1993, Dr. Willett and associates published in *Lancet* the results of a study that tracked almost 90,000 women. The study found a greater than 50% heart disease risk among those who ate higher trans fat foods such as margarine (in Gittleman, 1996). Additionally, research by Dr. Mary Enig warned us that trans fats are implicated in rising cancer rates, lower immunity, obesity, increased insulin levels, and a compromised ability to detoxify drugs and chemicals in the body (Gittleman, 2002).

These fats are truly the bad fats. However, there are also some good fats that are essential for the hungry brain.

## BRAIN JOGGER

Have students bring in food package labels from home for a couple of weeks. Do not tell them why they are doing so. Place the labels in a shoebox or other container. After you feel they have a large enough sample, place the students in groups of three.

Jobs:

Material manager: Divides the labels into equal numbers and distributes them to each group.

Recorder: Records the frequency of the food eaten throughout the designated time period by group members.

Timer: Watches the clock to ensure timely completion of the task.

The group must then look at each label it received, and tally the number of times group members have consumed that food in the past week or two. The recorder writes the tallies on the paper. This should take about ten minutes.

Then compare and contrast the foods the students have eaten. Which foods are the most popular? The least popular?

For the second part of the lesson, now have them look at the most popular foods first. How many of these foods contain partially hydrogenated oils? Ask around the room to name and list the foods that contain the bad brain food fats.

For a class or group project, have students target a food manufacturer and write to the company to see if it will disclose the reason for including hydrogentated fat in the food's preparation.

# Avoiding Trans Fats

One of the fats that will become stiff and rigid in the brain is trans fat, or hydrogenated fat. These fats are to be avoided in a healthy diet. (Remember that the pliable fats are the good fats that better facilitate the communication between brain cells.) These stiff fats are by far the most dangerous fats that either a child or adult can consume.

> Reading food labels helps to identify the foods that contain trans fats.

Trans fats are most often found in processed packaged foods. Reading food labels helps to identify the foods that contain trans fats. If the food package label contains anything that reads, "partially hydrogenated any kind of fat," this translates to trans fats or unnatural fats that are harmful to humans and especially to our brains. The words "partially hydrogenated oil" appear on many popular foods children eat, including candies, cookies, cakes, crackers, nut butters, margarines, frozen dinners, pretzels, chips, chocolates, and many other items.

Hydrogenation is an unnatural process and one that creates the most harmful fats. Manufacturers usually begin the method of hydrogenation with the least expensive oils – soy, corn, or cottonseed. Often these oils are already rancid from the extraction process. These oils are also mixed with tiny metal particles, usually nickel oxide. Nickel oxide is toxic when absorbed and is impossible to totally eliminate from margarine. The oil is then mixed with hydrogen gas in a high-pressure, high-temperature reactor. Next, soap-like emulsifiers and starch are squeezed into the mixture to give it a better consistency. Then the oil is cleaned with steam to remove the bad odor. Does this sound like a process you want done to your food?

Of special concern are the high amounts of trans fats in peanut butters. Some children eat nothing but peanut butter every day. The popular, easy to spread brands are loaded with partially hydrogenated oils. They also have extra sugar added to enhance the flavor. One of the reasons food manufacturers add partially hydrogenated oils to food products is to increase shelf life and, in the case of peanut butter and margarine, to make them spreadable like butter. There is no nutritional reason to add these unnatural partially hydrogenated fats to foods. Food companies add them simply for marketing reasons.

Something to remember when buying nut butters that do not contain hydrogenated fats is to look for the brands where a little bit of oil rises to the top of the jar and forms a layer. This layer is easily stirred into the nut butter when you open the jar at home. Once the jar is open then it is best to refrigerate it. Some stores even place their non-hydrogenated brands of peanut butter in the refrigerated section of the store. Included in your choice of nut butters that are good for you and your children are the sugar free brands.

It is alarming to see the number of processed food items children eat that contain partially hydrogenated oils. Just pick up a food package label from almost any snack food and, chances are, you will see the words "partially hydrogenated oil." Remember, this translates into trans fats, the most dangerous type of fat you can eat. Teach your students to avoid foods that contain any amount of partially hydrogenated oils. These oils are the brain's nemesis.

## DID YOU KNOW?

The whole of Europe has had mandates against trans fats for some years. Many European countries actually ban the use of trans fats altogether. In the United States, however, trans fats abound. The popularity of fast and convenient foods in America is overwhelming. The hydrogenation of oils affords those food companies that process their food a longer shelf life, and that translates into dollars.

# Blood Supply and Fat

Another important way the fat we eat affects the brain is through the brain's blood supply. The essential fatty acids that make up the membranes of the nerves also make up the membranes of the blood vessels. Fatty acid imbalance can set the structural tone of the vessel walls.

The same essential fatty acids affect the formation of messengers that influence blood vessel spasm. Chemicals called prostacyclins are produced when a child or adult consumes the right balance of fatty acids. Prostacyclins tend to relax blood vessels, desirable to maintain oxygen flow to the brain. These messengers help prevent the constriction of blood vessels and maintain a rich supply of oxygen to the brain (Schmidt, 1997).

Another way in which fat affects the brain's blood supply is by changing blood viscosity, or thickness. Although blood seems watery, it is actually rich with millions of cells and molecules. Blood becomes thicker, or sludge-like, when some of the formed elements stick together. The elements that stick together are called platelets, tiny little microscopic cells that drift in the sea of blood. When arachiconic acid (a fat from meat and dairy products) gets too high, its products (thromboxanes) signal the blood platelets to clump together when and where you do not want them to clump, a process that can adversely influence blood flow to the brain. Anything that might cause the blood to thicken threatens to interfere with the delivery of needed oxygen, nutrients and raw materials to a site.

When certain blood fats get too high, they make blood thicker. The higher the fat level, the thicker the blood. As the blood becomes thicker it may slow oxygen to the brain and affect its function. The result may be changes in mood and behavior. The typical fats involved in making the blood fatter and more viscous are triglycerides and cholesterol.

Triglycerides are fats attached to a glycerol molecule, which is made up of three fatty acids. They are essentially the major transport and storage vehicle for fats in our bodies.

As reported in a study published by Dr. Glueck in 1994, he discovered that depressed patients had a familial form of hyperlipidemia (elevated blood fats). In an interview *in Psychology Today*, he stated, "we have shown that, in patients with high triglycerides who were in a depressive state, the more you lower the triglycerides the more you alleviate the depression" (Carper, 2001). Other researchers have found that modifying blood fats can influence hostility, aggression, and contribute to a domineering attitude and other aspects of mood.

### DID YOU KNOW?

- Fat is a nutrient.
- There are fats that are good for you and fats that must be avoided for good health.
- We need a certain amount of good fat in our diet to feed our hungry brain.
- Good fats (Omega-3, Omega-6, and Omega-9) will not clog arteries.
- Fat is nine calories per gram.
- Butter is better than margarine.
- The Mediterranean diet is high in olive oil (Omega-9).
- Ocean fish, flax seed oil and walnuts are high in Omega-3 fatty acid.
- Plants are high in Omega-6 fatty acid.
- Olive oil, avocados, and almonds are high in Omega-9 nonessential fatty acid.
- Every cell of our body is made up of a fat coating. The fat acts as a barrier to keep out harmful microbes.

- The human brain, the most complex organization of matter, is 60% fat.
- Fat maintains the integrity of neuron connections in the brain's vital communication system.
- Nerve, brain, eye, heart, and adrenal and thyroid cells must have essential fats to function.
- Fat is required for the production of serotonin, which elevates mood and promotes good sleep (Ross 1999).
- Shortage of essential fats reduces effectiveness of vitamins A, D, E, and K.
- Trans fats, or partially hydrogenated fats, are the most unhealthy type of fat and should be avoided in a healthy diet.

 **BRAIN JOGGER**

Study the people of the Mediterranean region and determine what they eat. Research what diseases are prevalent. Find out from which diseases they die. E-mail someone in a Mediterranean country. Ask, what do children your age eat for lunch in that region? What do they eat for breakfast?

Construct a Venn diagram of good fats and bad fats.

Have the children bring in food labels for one week. Let them bring in labels from favorite foods from home and the school cafeteria. Pile them up in a fun place in the room, but do not tell the kids why they are collecting the labels.

When finished with the collection, place students in groups of three. Distribute the labels to the groups. As them to discover the food products that contain hydrogenated fats.

In cooperative groups write to the food giants and ask them why they use these fats.

Compare butter to margarine in a Venn diagram. Let both just sit there and see what happens when real food perishes.

Pre-school: Make butter; try to make margarine.

Chart and graph how many different types of nuts the class has eaten.

Chart and graph the types of fish eaten.

# BRAIN FOOD LESSONS

## What We Know

### An Elementary Lesson

## Focus Activity

Ask the class what the word nutrition means to them. Sample several children. Ask the class to fill in the analogy: "Gas is to a _____ as good food is to our bodies." Ask the class to explain: How is nutrition like school?

## Activity

Place the students in groups of three. Assign roles of: material manager, recorder, and reporter. Have a model of a KWL chart on the board. Have the material manager gather a sheet of newsprint, and the markers.

# K W L

This chart stands for what our group "Knows" about nutrition, what they "Want" to know about nutrition, and what they "Learned" about nutrition after the lesson. Instruct them to work on the "K" part first. They can each take a turn and share what they know about nutrition. The recorder writes the response on the newsprint. After a few minutes stop them and have the reporters read what their group knows about nutrition. Now move on to the "W" part and have the recorder write what they want to know about nutrition. Again, let the reporters share with the entire class.

## Reflection

Have the groups complete this statement: The reason we are studying nutrition is _____. Facilitate a class discussion around this question.

# On the way to my heart

## Intermediate and Middle School Lesson

## Focus Activity

Have the students begin to bring in food labels from all of the their favorite foods: candy wrappers, chip packets, and so on. Do not tell them why, just start collecting as a class. This will take about a week. Tell the class the only criteria for the label is it must be a food that they really like. After a week's worth of collecting, begin this focus activity.

As a class, make three lists on the board:

Sort the food labels into these food categories:

- Food to die for
- Food we like a lot
- Food we can live without

Have three students come up to the board and stand under each list with a piece of chalk in their hand. Tell them they must vote for each food held up by the teacher, and they must put them in one of the three categories. Even the three students at the board must vote.

The voting should look like this: The teacher holds up the first label, for example a package of Doritos. The teacher writes Doritos on the far left side of the list .The teacher than says, "how many of you put Doritos in the 'to die for' category?" The student recorder standing at the board records the tallies. Then the teacher asks, "how many of you would put Doritos in the 'like it a lot' category?" And finally asks the class, "how many of you would put Doritos in the 'can do without if I had to' category?" Each time the student recorder records the tallies. Do this for each food. Discuss the results, and talk about what makes those popular foods so appealing to them. Ask them what they think their grandparents ate, and what people in other countries eat today.

## Activity

Have the students move into their nutrition groups of three.

Assign roles of: materials manager, recorder and timer.

The materials manager will gather the following materials: four food labels, ten straws (must be transparent straws), one plastic spoon, a teaspoon, a tablespoon, a bowl or cup with about one half cup of

Crisco in it (the material manager can measure out the Crisco for the group), one piece of colored paper (navy blue works well here, or any dark color except black).

Have a discussion about foods they like. Now, lets see about some of these popular foods.

Instruct each group to do the following:

Timers will give their groups 20 minutes for this task.

Recorders will record and rewrite on the dark-colored paper.

Tell them that one tablespoon is equal to about five grams of fat. As a team they are to look over the food package label for a serving size first and determine that. This can be tricky to find. Assist them in this by modeling one example of a serving size on one of the class labels. After they find the serving size on all four labels they proceed to the next step.

The material manager begins. They take a label and check the number of grams of saturated fat per serving size. Knowing that a tablespoon is approximately five grams, and that three teaspoons equal one tablespoon, the materials manager will measure out the amount of saturated fat for the particular food, and stuff it into the clear straw. They may need more than one straw on some very high fat foods. The recorder then writes the name of the food on the dark paper (using masking tape if the ink does not show up) and labels the food and the amount of grams of fat per serving. Take clear tape and tape the fat-filled straw to the paper under the information written about it.

Each group member takes a turn with one of the labels, and together they do the last (fourth) label. They perfect their finished product together (add color).

Come back together as a class, and have the timer report the findings, and to share their group reactions to what they found.

Now revisit the tallying that was done at the beginning of the period. Take the vote again.

## Reflection

Have each group finish these statements and share them with the class. Today we learned _____.
Today we decided _____.

# 'J' is for JUNK

## High School Lesson

## Focus Activity

Give each student a five by eight index card, and some markers or colored pencils. In the center have them write their first name. Tell them that you are going to give them a verbal direction and they are to draw their response on the proper space on the card. Tell them these responses should be in visual form only. No words!

Upper right corner: A visual representation of their favorite fast food restaurant.

Lower right corner: A visual of a couple of their favorite junk foods.

Lower left corner: A visual of their favorite vegetable.

Upper left corner: A visual of their favorite fruit.

Give them a couple of minutes to perfect their pictures. Instruct them to stand up and to approach someone in the class and exchange cards. Ask each other questions about the pictures. Spend a couple of minutes with that person, but no more. Instruct them to move on to another individual and spend a few moments with them, asking them questions about their card. Repeat this process a few more times. After about ten minutes, instruct them to sit down.

Ask the class to report on what they found as they walked around the room. Did they notice anything? What was the easiest response to draw? Why? What was the most difficult to draw? Why?

## Activity

Have the students move into groups of three. Assign roles of: recorder, timer, and material manager. The material manager will gather the materials consisting of: several markers of various colors, and two sheets of newsprint. Instruct them to share their cards with their team members, and to see if they have the same favorite fast food place to visit in common. What is a favorite junk food of the group? Have the group decide on a favorite fast food place, and a favorite junk food. After the threesome has decided, have the recorder create a wishbone graphic organizer for their fast food choice (see following). Have the group analyze the attributes of their groups favorite fast food restaurant.

## Reflection

What makes you go to that place? What's in it for you? What's in it for them? Who benefits the most?

# Chapter 4
## Sugar

*As you eat, so shall you think.*

*– Elizabeth Somer*

In the United States of America, sugar perhaps could have remained for us a sweet, harmless substance if its consumption had remained at a similar level to that consumed by our forefathers. But, like everything else, things change, including the availability of sugar. Today, sugar is all around us. Americans are consuming greater and greater quantities as we rely much more on packaged foods that contain a wide variety of sugar. The problem is our bodies were not designed to handle this sugar overload. But, boy, do we eat it! Most of us consume our weight in sugar every year.

> For centuries, people have found ample satisfaction in the sweetness of fruits.

For centuries, people have found ample satisfaction in the sweetness of fruits, berries, and some vegetables. Eastern Mediterranean peoples in biblical times used honey as an added sweetener, and prized it so highly that Canaan, the promised land of the Israelites, was lauded as "a land flowing with milk and honey." When Asian sugarcane was introduced into Europe in the middle ages, it was so rare and costly that druggists often sold it for medicinal purposes at prices only the wealthy could afford (Null, 1984).

Modern technology and big business have turned sugar and sugar products from luxury to commonplace items. In so doing, they have altered our health for the worse. Americans consume more calories than do poorer nations, but most of them come from fat and sugar. The people of poorer nations get roughly the same carbohydrate totals we do, but a greater quantity of theirs comes in the form of complex, unrefined carbohydrates. In this sense, ironically, they are healthier than we.

The word "sugar" can be confusing because its meaning is very broad. There are two types of carbohydrates: simple sugars – sucrose or table sugar – and complex carbohydrates, which we know as starches (such as potatoes), cereal, fruits, and other vegetables. Sucrose is refined table sugar. Fructose is sugar in fruits. Glucose is sugar in the blood. For the sake of clarity, sugar will be used as the term for white refined sugar. Blood sugar will be used to mean glucose, which is brain and muscle fuel.

> When kids consume empty calories, they crowd out room in their hungry brains for more nutritious foods.

Sugar as table sugar or sucrose has no value other than providing calories. The calories from sucrose are completely devoid of nutrients – containing no protein, minerals, vitamins or fiber – just simple carbohydrates that easily convert to fat. In order to digest sugar, the body requires the minerals chromium, manganese, cobalt, copper, zinc and magnesium. Since these minerals are lost in the sugar refining process, the human body has to draw upon and deplete its own supply of these nutrients in order to digest and metabolize the sugar (Appleton, 1988).

Too many empty calories in the diet can especially be a problem for school-aged children, as demonstrated by increasing childhood obesity rates. When kids consume empty calories, they crowd out room in their hungry brains for more nutritious foods. It's important for all of us, both children and adults, to make each calorie as nutrient-dense as possible to get the maximum benefit from the foods we eat.

Another consequence of eating too much sugar is a weakened immune system. Dr. Jacqueline Krohn, in her book, *The Whole Way to Allergy Relief and Prevention*, states that "sugar depletes the body of specific nutrients including B complex vitamins, magnesium, chromium and other minerals. Ingested sugar destroys the germ-killing capacities of the white blood cells for approximately four hours." When the immune system, the body's defense mechanism against disease, is depleted by the over-ingestion of sugar, this makes it easier for illness to strike (Krone, 1991).

Let's take a look at what the founders of this country ate in terms of sugar to illustrate how far we've come from healthy eating to our present unhealthy state. Since the beginning of this country, people ate sugar only occasionally as a rare and very special treat. Due in part to the unavailability of the sugar, they did not eat sugar in concentrated form.

Now sugar and other sweeteners abound in grocery stores and on our home food shelves. Sugar is the number one food additive used in the United States. The following chart shows the alarming rise in sugar consumption in America since the early 1800s.

Sugar Consumption per Person Each Year

| Year | Amount in Pounds |
|------|------------------|
| Early 1800s | 12 |
| 1850 | 22 |
| 1875 | 41 |
| 1895 | 63 |
| 1915 | 95 |
| 1935 | 115 |
| 1955 | 119 |
| 1976 | 125 |
| 1990 | 130–140 |

Source: Miller, Bruce, D.D.S., and James Scala, PhD, *Better Health* (Dallas, Texas: Miller Enterprises Inc., 1994)

The chart shows how the consumption of sweet sugary foods has gotten out of hand. When you add non-caloric sweeteners to the list, Americans are consuming almost 165 pounds of sugar annually (Gittleman, 1996). Contrast that to the 12 pounds we ate in the early 1800s and you can see that sugar consumption has risen more than 1,500% in the last two hundred years – a drastic change in our food supply system and in our eating habits.

# Sugar on the Brain

Some of us can handle eating sugary foods in larger amounts than others. But at least 16% of us have something called low blood sugar or glucose irregularities. Let's take a look at how this nutritional problem has an effect on children in school.

Mrs. Hernandez reports that Grant, a fourth-grader in her class, is an energetic learner in the morning when he enters her classroom. Around 10 a.m., however, Grant starts to get a little ornery, turning a little bit into a Jekyll and Hyde. Once he hit a friend on the playground just before lunch. He was sincerely remorseful afterwards and won his friend back. It just seemed this hitting behavior was out of character for Grant.

> Some of us can handle eating sugary foods in larger amounts than others.

Actually, what was happening to Grant happens to about 16% of the population. It's called low blood sugar. Out of 30 classroom children, 16% is about five students. What happens to these five low-blood-sugar kids by mid-morning? Their busy brains are not getting the proper fuel they need. When their stomachs are empty, their brain power diminishes, and this can lead to drowsiness, lack of concentration, change of personality, headaches, temper tantrums, panic attacks, and even blackouts.

The brain is a hungry, rapidly metabolizing organ, so brain fuel shortages create problems with concentration, mood and memory. There is no room for storage of fuel in the brain, so it needs nutrients and its main fuel, glucose, constantly flowing through it, especially during times of mental concentration.

Without glucose in the brain from the foods we eat, individuals may become unconscious and lapse into a coma. Nature in her wisdom has provided a backup system, however. When there is too little glucose in the bloodstream, the body releases a chemical to send more sugar into the bloodstream, preventing a coma. This chemical is called epinephrine or adrenaline. But the chemical epinephrine has its own unique effect on the body. Commonly known as adrenaline, epinephrine works on both the nervous and immune systems, affecting our hearts, lungs, brain and stomach.

> Adrenaline is referred to as the "fight-or-flight" hormone, necessary for protection in times of danger.

Adrenaline is referred to as the "fight-or-flight" hormone, necessary for protection in times of danger. The release of adrenaline, which happens when we are scared or feel we are in some sort of trouble, causes changes in our body that allow us to become more alert, and even stronger to better protect ourselves. Taking energy away from digestion, adrenaline allows us to transfer our energy into to running, fighting, or doing whatever else we must do to survive.

When adrenaline is dumped into a child's bloodstream to counteract the low blood sugar, the child feels the 'flight-or-fight' energy surge and may react unpredictably. Even if the student is sitting comfortably in the classroom trying to pay attention, an adrenaline release may have a profound effect. The pupils of their eyes may dilate and the heart rate may increase. A child in this state may not be capable of sitting still or paying attention. Any little thing might trigger the student to become agitated and act up.

Although adults can react in the same manner, this kind of experience is just more confusing for kids. It's the adrenaline release that causes the irritability, agitation and shakiness we feel when hungry. It's an especially uncomfortable feeling for children because they do not understand what's happening in their busy brains.

In her book *No More Ritalin: Treating ADHD Without Drugs*, Dr. Mary Ann Block states that low blood sugar (hypoglycemia) is the most significant underlying problem found with children who exhibit behavior problems. Symptoms are usually easy to identify in children, including agitation or irritability when he or she wakes up in the morning or before meals, becoming better after eating. In other words, the child with a Jekyll and Hyde behavior, who is sweet one minute and agitated, angry and irritable the next, may have hypoglycemia (Block, 1996).

By now you might be thinking, "What does all this have to do with eating sugar?" The answer is that the condition of hypoglycemia experienced by the fourth-grader, Grant, can be brought about in two different ways. One way to cause a low blood sugar state is by eating too many simple, high carbohydrate sugary foods. The other is from a lack of food to the brain caused by skipping meals. These two causes abound in school-aged children.

Let's look closely at the sugar paradox affecting Grant. It would appear that if a person consumes sugar, more sugar would get into the bloodstream, not less, but this is not the case. What happens? When sugar and refined carbohydrates (white bread, pasta, crackers, cereal, etc.) are eaten without protein or fiber, they are quickly converted to glucose in the bloodstream. This can happen in a matter of minutes. The high glucoses levels then signal the body to produce large amounts of insulin to process the glucose and reduce blood sugar levels. The flood of insulin results in a bottoming out of blood sugar, leaving little supply for the brain. The brain is deprived of its fuel.

■ □ ■ □ ■

In this case, Grant has low blood sugar from not having enough food to fuel his brain as opposed to consuming a high-sugar diet. This can be corrected by eating small, frequent meals throughout the course of the day, so Mrs. Hernandez and Grant's mom decided to make sure Grant ate a mid-morning snack. A list was sent home to his parents as to what would be acceptable. Some of the suggestions included:

- Apples
- Bananas
- Yogurt
- Celery with peanut butter
- All vegetables
- A chicken leg
- Part of his lunch
- Whole grain bread with cheese or nut butter
- Nuts
- Whole grain crackers.

Absent from the list were sugary, non-food items such as soft drinks, cookies, cake, doughnuts, chips and candy. Instead, fruits and vegetables were sent to school with Grant, and the plan worked! Everyone was happy – Mrs. Hernandez, Grant's parents and, most of all, Grant.

Grant's teacher was definitely on to something. Smart Mrs. Hernandez used snack time to teach her students how too many sugary foods depleted the brain of the important fuel it needs. She taught them the difference between junk food and real food. She highly praised them when good nutrition choices were made in the lunchroom. She noticed students from other homerooms trying to elicit praise for their lunches. Soon she developed a reputation as the "good food police" and several other teachers asked her to teach them about the mid-morning snack.

Julia Ross, in her book, *The Diet Cure*, writes about sugar:

When white sugar was first introduced to Europe in the 16th century, it was kept under lock and key because of its potency. It was worth its weight in silver and they even called it "crack"!

Just because sugar is legal, cheap, and easily available doesn't mean it isn't destructive. Remember, cocaine was once the key ingredient in Coca-Cola, and available to adults and children all across America ( Ross, 1999, p. 45).

# Low Blood Sugar

If you have low blood sugar, you probably know it. You can't skip a meal without suffering because your brain will start to falter when your stomach is empty. You might even shake because you haven't eaten in a couple of hours. Perhaps diabetes runs in your family, or perhaps you come from a family with a history of alcoholism. These are factors to consider if you think you may be suffering from low blood sugar. Here are some symptoms:

## Symptoms of Low Blood Sugar

- History of feeling faint or having blackouts
- Constant hungry feeling
- Chronic fatigue or tiredness
- Shakiness or irritability after missing a meal
- Craving for sweets
- Drowsiness after missing meals
- Family history of diabetes
- Family history of alcoholism
- Headache when meals are missed
- Moodiness

- Preference for carbohydrate foods
- Moodiness relieved by eating
- Irritability
- Depression
- Aggressiveness
- Insomnia
- Nervousness
- Vertigo
- Dizziness
- Lack of concentration
- Indecisiveness

# Kids and Sugar

Most kids love their sugary foods (as do most adults, too); they're part of our culture. But children seem to be more sensitive to the onslaught of sugar in their bodies than adults are. The child's busy brain is not only hungry for knowledge, but for good nutrition as well. Too much sugar can interfere with the blood glucose level that is so important for optimal brain functioning – especially in children.

> The child's busy brain is not only hungry for knowledge, but for good nutrition as well.

A study conducted at Yale University in 1995 investigated the effects of sugar on adults and children. Each group was fed a certain amount of sugar. Blood glucose levels and blood adrenaline levels were measured every half hour for five hours. The blood sugar levels remained normal in both adults and children, indicating the adrenaline was doing its job of keeping glucose levels normal. However, adrenaline levels in the children were ten times higher than normal for up to five hours after ingesting the sugar. All of the children in the study had symptoms of increased adrenaline while only one of the adults did (Jones, et al., 1995).

It appears from this study that children are more susceptible than adults to the ill effects of sugar. The study was conducted on "normal" children. An even more pronounced reaction to sugar occurs in children who have a chemical imbalance in their brains.

Another study implicates sugary foods as having a deleterious effect on behavior and learning. In the spring of 1979, the New York City board of education ordered a reduction in the sugar content of foods served in the school lunch and breakfast programs, and banned two artificial food colorings. The study involved 803 schools. At the time of the study, New York ranked in the 39th percentile on the California Achievement Test (CAT). In 1980 of the following year, test scores soared to the 47th percentile. By the spring of 1983, CAT scores had risen to the national 55th percentile, a build-up reflecting dietary changes over the study's three years. No other district had reported a large increase so quickly within such a large population (Schoenthaler, Doraz, Wakefield, 1986).

Before the New York schools' dietary changes, the more school food consumed, the worse the children performed academically. After the quality of food was improved, the more school food consumed, the better the children performed academically. The shift in the relationship between eating school food and academic performance seems to be clearly linked to changes in the quality of the food.

The authors concluded that the primary cause of the academic gains in 803 New York City public schools compared to the rest of the United States, significantly surpassing the rest of the nation, was probably due to the reduction in malnutrition. Dietary revisions provided more vitamins, minerals and amino acids to students. Wholesome food thus translated into a powerful academy tool for children in school.

> More studies convince us that the idea of good nutrition ought to be taken seriously.

■ □ ■ □ ■

More studies convince us that the idea of good nutrition ought to be taken seriously. Twelve juvenile correctional facilities in three states reported a 48% decline in violence and general antisocial behavior in more than 7,000 young people following the implementation of new diet policies, as high sugar foods were replaced with fruits, vegetables, and wholegrain products (Schoenthaler, 1983).

## Sugar Shack Shambles

We all know by now that most sugary foods are empty calorie foods, meaning they have little or no nutritional value. Most pastries, cookies, cakes and candies are comprised of fat and sugar. If children consumed these foodless foods once in a while, in conjunction with more nutritious foods, little harm would accrue for most of them. However, children are eating two, three and sometimes four times their own body weight in sugar annually. This comes to about five-and-a-half ounces per child, per day, and about 130 pounds of sugar per person, per year (Simontacchi, 2000). If a youngster is consuming that much sugar, there is little room left for the more nutritious foods the child really needs.

We know that individuals whose glandular system – the pancreas, pituitary, thyroid and adrenal glands – is not operating properly have difficulty in controlling blood sugar, and that they are very sensitive to excessive sugar in the diet. Excess dietary sugar amplifies the problem of blood sugar regulation in the body.

Stress on the endocrine system is another way in which dietary sugar can have an adverse impact on our brains and bodies (Bland, 1996).

In 1990, Dr. Allan Zametkin published results of a trial in the *New England Journal of Medicine*. In his study, Dr. Zametkin found that errors of sugar metabolism occurred in adults with ADD and ADHD. More importantly, glucose metabolism in the ADD/ADHD brain was lowest in the prefrontal part of the brain, the section that regulates behavior, impulsivity, and attention (in Zimmerman, 1999). Excess intake of sugary foods can thus increase the problem of blood sugar regulation.

Our bodies have not yet adapted to a high consumption of refined carbohydrates such as sugar. Only during the past one to two hundred years have we eaten sugar in such large quantities. One hundred years ago the average sugar intake was about four pounds per person, per year. Today the average intake is about 130 pounds per person, per year. Sugar is the number one food preservative added to today's food supply. Prove it to yourself by checking out the food package labels on your shelf. Most of them will probably contain some type of sugar.

Over the course of human existence glucose has been provided by the slow release of sugar from complex carbohydrates. This slow release delays the insulin response. Our bodies are well adapted to handling a slower and more controlled release of glucose. A rapid rise in glucose, which occurs when too much sugar is consumed, is interpreted by the body as a dangerous, life-threatening situation.

Bonnie Spring, Ph.D., a researcher at Texas Tech University in Lubbock, Texas, found some interesting results in children who ate a high carbohydrate breakfast (in Zimmerman, 1999). She discovered these children scored poorly on attention tests in comparison to children who had no breakfast. Those who had eaten a high protein breakfast did much better than those who either ate no breakfast or ate a breakfast high in carbohydrates. The group of children who ate a high carbohydrate breakfast was affected quickly, within 30 minutes after they ate. The effect lasted for four hours.

In another study conducted at the Yale University School of Medicine and published in October of 1995 in the *Journal of Pediatric Research*, 17 ADHD children and 11 children without ADHD were given a glucose beverage before eating breakfast. Glucose is a simple sugar made from dietary sugars and other carbohydrates. The amount of glucose was about the amount of sugar you would find in a large sweet roll, a large glass of orange juice, and a cup of coffee with two rounded teaspoons of sugar. That's about eight times the amount of sugar the brain requires in a single hour. Both groups of children exhibited an expected jump in blood glucose levels within the first half hour (Girardi, 1995). The increase in blood glucose in the children tested was countered by a rapid rise in blood insulin levels. Insulin's role is to move glucose from the circulating system into the cells where it will be stored as a sugar complex called glycogen. Most of our cells have the capacity to store extra glucose and save it for later energy needs. But the brain cells do not have the ability to store any glucose. The brain takes what little glucose it can immediately use, but even this meager amount may be severely restricted if insulin levels are high. The body, in its wisdom, has a way to guard against the deficits in brain glucose: the adrenal glands.

Within three hours of eating a sugary meal, blood glucose levels drop back to normal or slightly below normal. This decrease in glucose triggers another important event that affects brain chemistry involving the adrenal glands. Two tiny organs on top of the kidneys, the adrenals, produce the "fight-or-flight" hormones epinephrine and norepinephrine. These hormones step up glucose entry into the brain, which offsets the effects of insulin.

In both groups of children tested, glucose and insulin levels dropped within three hours, as expected, but what Girardi and his colleagues found when they checked epinephrine and norepinephrine levels was quite telling.

The ADHD children showed a 50% lower rise in these counterbalancing hormones as compared to their non-ADHD counterparts. The children diagnosed with ADHD were less able to counteract the stressful effects on their brains of the high-sugar meal. These findings are of great interest to teachers and parents of ADHD children. Since norepinephrine is a neurotransmitter that raises alertness and the flow of information between brain cells, a boost in brain functioning will be especially critical to those already sensitive (and probably suffering) children diagnosed with ADHD.

You probably already know how addictive sugar can be. Just try living without it. Although we know cookies, candies, cakes and other confections are worthless nutritionally, we can't seem to stop eating them. If you could stop eating sugary foods on your own, you probably would. Just imagine how a small child feels, since you yourself have probably failed at "just saying no" to sugar. But for the child with sensitive brain chemistry, sugar can be dangerous to learning and behavior.

## How Kids Are Seduced by Sugar

Beyond the Internet, there is a world of marketing targeted to kids. Forget about childhood being a time of carefree pleasure. Corporate America is targeting our children, as marketers today grab kids before they can walk and talk, indoctrinating them with messages to buy, buy, buy.

Let's explore a day in the life of a nine-year-old. We'll call her Anna. While Anna gobbles her breakfast of Pokémon cold cereal, she plays with the plastic McDonald's restaurant that Mattel has created for Barbie. In the meantime, Barbie's sister, Skipper, visits the restaurant wearing an outfit covered with Pepsi logos.

Now it's off to school. Anna's teacher uses materials created by McDonald's to teach a lesson on the environment. Anna and her classmates make food chain wheels, study about problems with trash, and start their own recycling project using the activity sheets that carry the McDonald's logo.

It's time for lunch. In the school cafeteria, Anna gets to choose from hamburgers, french fries, pizza, deep fried chicken nuggets, chocolate milk, cookies, ice-cream sandwiches, and other popular foods. It's hard to tell if you are not in a fast food restaurant. That's because some school authorities believe it is more important to succeed financially than to teach and model good nutrition. It is sometimes believed that kids will only eat something resembling fast food. This may or may not be true. But schools should be places that model "what should be" and proper nutrition is crucial to human health.

> Schools should be places that model "what should be" and proper nutrition is crucial to human health.

After lunch it's back to class to listen to a guest speaker from popular fast food restaurant who's speaking as part of the restaurant's "Adopt-a-School" program. The speaker presents awards to outstanding students.

Another big event occurs during the last hour of the school's schedule. That's when another popular fast food pizza place delivers pizzas for the whole class. The party is part of the restaurant's "Book Club!" program that rewards students for reading a certain number of books. The students receive certificates for free pizzas.

Back home after school, Anna turns on the TV and watches cartoons: *Gummy Bears*, *Pokémon* and *Tiny Toon Adventures*. It's hard for her to separate the programs from the commercials. That's because *Gummy Bears* was a spin off from a candy. While Anna watches, she chews on Garfield and Friends Chewy Fruit Snacks. Never mind that they contain no fruit!

Anna sees dozens of commercials. Most push fast food, sugared cereals, and candy. Anna enjoys the fast foods ads, since she's playing with a toy from one of them. The cooking center, produced by a popular toy company, has a pretend fry warmer, a deep fryer and a grill. For her birthday Anna is hoping for the Soda Fountain to make her restaurant complete.

Selling to kids is big business, and the food companies are good at it. Their tools range from "educational materials" to kids' clubs to massive, widespread television advertising campaigns. In the old days, marketers just targeted children with ads for traditional children's products such as toys. Advertisers now are promoting products to children that aren't strictly child-oriented.

Children today are basically being sold on foodless food from every direction. The fast food industry has a hold on our youth and it appears to be working. According to the Bogalusa Heart Study, children as young as three years old have fatty streaks in their arteries – a precursor to arteriosclerosis and heart disease. Obesity is now an epidemic in children and adolescents and seems to be on the rise (Simontacchi, 2000). Estimates on the percentage of children who are overweight range from 10% to 30%, and, as they grow older they grow fatter. Over the last 20 years the likelihood of being overweight has almost doubled in some age categories, with close to five million youths aged six to seventeen seriously overweight or obese (Physicians Committee for Responsible Medicine, 2004).

> Obesity is now an epidemic in children and adolescents and seems to be on the rise (Simontacchi, 2000).

# Helping Children Overcome the Sugar Monster

Believe it or not, there are some helpful things a person can do to overcome the "sugar monster."

Believe it or not, there are some helpful things a person can do to overcome the "sugar monster." The classroom teacher and some willing parents can teach and model good information and alternative eating habits for kids that promote good thinking and lifelong health. Even without the assistance of parents, schools can teach that health, like learning, is a lifelong endeavor.

First, let's find out if you are a carbohydrate-addicted person. Here is a test devised by Dr. Joan Mathews Larson, the author of *Seven Weeks to Sobriety: The Proven Program to Fight Alcoholism through Nutrition* (Mathews Larson, 1998).

Teachers and parents may take the test for themselves and observe these behaviors in children. Older children who can read and write can take the test themselves.

Take the Carbohydrate Addiction test formulated by Dr. Joan Mathews Larson:

| Y/N | | Question |
|---|---|---|
| | 1. | When eating sweets, starches or snack foods, is it hard to stop? |
| | 2. | At a restaurant, do you eat several rolls or bread before the meal is served? |
| | 3. | Do you ever hide food or eat food secretly? |
| | 4. | While eating carbohydrates, do you ever feel out of control? |
| | 5. | Does your diet consist mainly of breads, pastas, starchy vegetables, fast foods, or sweets? |
| | 6. | Do you binge on snack foods, candy or fast foods? |

| | 7. | Does eating a sweet snack food lift your spirits? |
|---|---|---|
| | 8. | Do you feel hungry and unsatisfied after a meal no matter how much you eat? |
| | 9. | Do you feel sleepy or groggy after a high-carbohydrate meal? |
| | 10. | Which would you prefer |

| spaghetti | steak |
|---|---|
| sandwich | salad |
| potato | broccoli |
| cookie | strawberries |
| cracker | raw vegetables |
| chips | raw nuts |
| breaded fish | baked fish |

For question 10, consider your response a "yes" if you checked more items in the left-hand column than in the right-hand column.

Score:

Total the number of "yes" responses. Then determine which of the following categories you fit into:

1–2   doubtful addiction

3–4   mild addiction

5–6   moderated addiction

7–10  severe addiction

If you scored more than 5, you are a candidate for a low-carb diet and will want to restrict carbohydrates from 50 to 75 grams daily.

One very helpful way to decrease sugar cravings is to eat breakfast. Not just anything, though. A breakfast of protein is the best way, and really the only good way, for a child with a big sweet tooth to begin the day. Protein performs so many good things for the body that it is suggested for all individuals even if they don't have a sugar problem.

Protein is brain food. It literally feeds the brain the food it needs. The brain requires amino acids, which it can only obtain from protein. The amino acids the brain needs for alertness are tyrosine and phenelalanine. These help to manufacture dopamine and norepinephrine, the alertness neurotransmitters. Protein also tells the brain the body is full, in other words nourished, and helps to balance blood sugar so important for brain functioning. And it keeps the gut full longer, so hunger does not set in and distract learning.

> Protein is brain food. It literally feeds the brain the food it needs.

Julia Ross explains in her book, *The Diet Cure*, that protein malnutrition causes brain power outage. "As the activity of the brain shrinks with dieting, the brain's mental and emotional stability can falter and even fail" (Ross, 1999). Dieting usually means low fat and low protein. Since brain and mood chemicals can only be made from protein, moods and thinking can deteriorate without enough of this mind food.

A protein breakfast usually should replace an unhealthy, high carbohydrate breakfast, such as a bagel or toast of white bread. Even worse is cold, sugary cereal with cow's milk, a common allergen. Eggs and whole wheat toast would be a much better choice. A protein breakfast will help keep blood sugar balanced throughout the school day.

> A protein breakfast usually should replace an unhealthy, high carbohydrate breakfast, such as a bagel or toast of white bread.

A ten o'clock snack is another healthful solution schools can adopt to help students.

## BRAIN JOGGER

Have the students bring in food labels for one week, but do not say why. Just collect them and place them in a box. Distribute the labels randomly to students sitting in pairs. Have the pairs of students select the different words for sugar. Some of them are glucose, dextrose, dextrin, maltodextrin, honey, sucrose, maltose, lactose, maple sugar, corn syrup, corn starch, corn sweetener, turbanodo sugar, sugar cane, sugar beet and confectioners glaze.

As a class, discuss the hidden sugars.

Bring in 5 oz. (150 g) of sugar and ask, "where is the hidden sugar in these foods?" Seeing the amount of sugar eaten per person, per day is a great visual aid for students.

Research the Internet for a farmer of sugar cane. What are the problems? What are the benefits of growing sugar cane? Why is sugar cane so mineral-hungry?

## DID YOU KNOW?

The average American consumes 139 lbs. of refined sugar each year that, if converted by the body, would make 79 lbs. of fat (Wild Oats publication, 2000).

No friend to the earth, white sugar production is a notorious polluter and resource-depleter. Sugar cane is a mineral-hungry plant known for soil depletion. Cane farming also requires massive amounts of chemical fertilizers and pesticides.

Brown sugar is simply refined sugar sprayed with molasses to make it appear more whole.

Turbanodo sugar is just one step away from white sugar. It only skips the final filtration stage of sugar refining, with little difference in nutrition.

High fructose corn syrup is a cheap and plentiful sweetener often used in soft drinks, candy and baked goods. It is similar to refined sugar in composition and effect.

If you must eat something that contains a lot of sugar, make certain you eat that food with a protein, such as fish, eggs, chicken, or beef.

A breakfast high in sugar (cereal) can be harmful to some children. Protein for breakfast is the way to go for brain power!

## Non-sugared Sweeteners

During the late 1960s and early 1970s the Twiggy generation was created. Twiggy (not her real name) was a bone-thin female fashion model from England who embodied everything hip during that time. After all, the Beatles were from England, so it seemed that everything British was "hip and cool." Twiggy's popularity stemmed from this culture. The late '60s and early '70s launched the waif-thin look with its unhealthy obsession with skinniness that had a great influence on teenage girls at the time. Twiggy was thinner than the supermodels of today. This was the look that was "in."

In an attempt to get thin, Americans were avoiding sugar and turning to non-sugar sweeteners. At the time of Twiggy and the Beatles, the most popular non-sugar sweetener was saccharin. Saccharin is a petroleum derivative that is a co-carcinogen, a promoter of other cancer causing agents in the body. For this very reason, its use has been prohibited in foods in France and Germany for almost a century.

The chemical name for this product is aspartame. Aspartame was introduced in the early 1980s and is much more expensive than table sugar, costing about $30 dollars a pound compared to 30¢ a pound for table sugar. Artificial sweeteners containing aspartame are sold under various trade names. Aspartame is about 200 times sweeter than table sugar and it intensifies the taste of other flavors and sweeteners. Shortly after its introduction, the Centers for Disease Control (CDC) published the results of a study they conducted in 1983. This study resulted from consumer complaints and concerns associated with food products containing aspartame. These complaints involved upsets to the central nervous and digestive systems and gynecological problems. Some of the problems reported were: mood changes, insomnia, seizures, abdominal pain, nausea and diarrhea. Also, irregular menses in women were reported (Zimmerman, 1999). Large amounts of aspartame consumed over time can upset the amino acid and neurotransmitter balance on the body. Another aspartame-related problem is that it tends to remove chromium from the body. Chromium is a trace mineral we need in our diet to maintain the brain's blood sugar levels. Indeed, chromium is a critical nutrient for the hungry brain. Some food sources of chromium include broccoli, meat, whole wheat, shellfish, brewer's yeast, nuts and egg yolks.

Aspartame, the main ingredient in artificial sweeteners used today, is chemically synthesized. Made from two amino acids, phenylalanine and aspartic acid, aspartame is bound together with methanol. Methanol is wood alcohol. An excess of methanol can cause blindness and even death (Peskin, 1999). Heat increases the rate of aspartame's conversion to methanol. Often cans of diet soft drinks are left in the sun or in warm trucks transported before they reach the soft drink machine or the buyer's kitchen table. Methanol must be metabolized by the liver in the same manner as ethanol, the alcohol found in wine, beer and spirits. For adults and teenagers consuming diet mixers with alcoholic drinks, methanol in the mixer adds additional work for the liver. Methanol is produced in small amounts by bacteria in the digestive system. The amount produced is normally not at all harmful; however, if additional methanol is ingested, the potential for toxicity, especially in children, is alarmingly increased.

The two remaining components that make up artificial sweetener – phenylalanine and aspartic acid – are not without side effects, either. William Pardridge, M.D., of the UCLA Department of Medicine, explained their effects in a paper titled, Potential Effects of the Dipeptide Sweetener Aspartame on the Brain, published in *Nutrition and the Brain, vol. 7.*

He found that the entry of aspartic acid into the brain is slowed down because of the blood brain barrier. However, phenylalanine readily crossed the blood brain barrier and converted within the neurons into the excitatory neurotransmitters norepinephrine and dopamine. If the blood is delivering to the brain more phenylalanine than other amino acids, the natural balance of neurotransmitters is upset. The neurotransmitters crowded out are the calming and stabilizing ones. As a result, symptoms that occur may include insomnia, short attention span, hyperactivity, hormone changes, decreased agility, and seizures in those with a family history of them. According to Dr. Pardridge, a quart or more per day of beverages containing artificial sweetener can result in alarming levels of phenylalanine. Remember that a quart is just four standard cups. If kids are eating snacks containing artificial sweeteners, these also can help ratchet up the alarming quantities of phenylalanine in the brain.

# More Reasons to Avoid Artificial Sweeteners

Doctor Russell Blaylock in his 1997 book, *Excitotoxins: the Taste That Kills*, calls aspartate, the main component of one popular artificial sweetener, an excitotoxin. Excitoxins are a group of excitory amino acids that can cause sensitive neurons to die. Excitotoxins also do damage by unleashing free radicals within the neurons. Free radicals are highly reactive substances that can damage important parts of a cell. Scientifically they consist of atoms or compounds having an unpaired valence electron in their outer orbital. Examples include hydroxyl ions and superoxide.

Dr. Blaylock states:

"High levels of excitotoxins within the brain appear to play a major role in Alzheimer's Disease. It is essential that individuals with a strong family history of Alzheimer's Disease, and those having had a stroke or high blood pressure, avoid excitotoxin food additives. The simplest way to do this is to restrict foods from your diet that contain excitotoxin taste enhancers such as MSG, hydrolyzed vegetable protein, and aspartame."

It is reported that aspartame problems account for more than 80% of all of the FDA food-related complaints. There are about 5,000 products on the market in the United States that contain aspartame. Keep in mind that aspartame serves only one purpose: to enhance the taste of food. It is not a preservative that keeps food from spoiling and has no nutritional value. It cannot feed the hungry brain.

> Keep in mind that aspartame serves only one purpose: to enhance the taste of food.

More scientific work convinces this author that artificial sweeteners are not in the best health interest of anyone, especially children. Reynolds and others discovered as early as 1976 that there is ample experimental evidence that glutamate found in MSG and aspartame found in artificial sweeteners both effect the neurological development of the hypothalamus. The hypothalamus is the midbrain or part of the limbic system that controls emotions, body temperature, hunger, thirst and sex drive. This means that these two excitotoxins can alter the way cells and pathways in the hypothalamus develop. This may result in permanent alteration of the anatomy, as well as the function, of the brain (Reynolds et al., in Blaylock, 1997).

Going cold turkey on diet soda is enough to send chills down the spines of many of us. Dr. John Lee's newsletter comments that one of the reasons we may love our diet soda so much:

"...maybe (because) they're loaded with caffeine and the artificial sweetener aspartame, which is both a stimulant and an 'excitotoxin.' An excitotoxin excites or over-stimulates brain cells to the point where it kills them. Aspartame can cause dozens of possible side effects, including seizures.

To add insult to injury (literally), diet sodas have never been proven to help with weight loss. The reason for this is that the sweet taste of the diet soda sends a signal to the brain that sugar is coming. And the brain sends a signal to the pancreas to make insulin, the hormone that will usher the sugar out of the blood stream and into the pancreas and into your cells. This will stimulate your appetite, so you'll eat more, and insulin also sends signals to convert sugar to fat. It's a no-win situation" (Lee, 1998: p. 7).

---

### DID YOU KNOW?

Diet soda belongs to my third food group, junk food. There is no deficiency of artificial sweeteners in the human body that has yet been reported in medical literature. This chemical cuisine is, at best, frivolous and unnecessary for human health.

---

■ □ ■ □ ■

Dr. Skye Weintraub reminds us in her book, *Natural Treatment for ADD and Hyperactivity* (1997), that sugar-free products may adversely affect low blood sugar conditions. This information is critical for the hungry brain. Aspartame can make hypoglycemia worse, especially because of the severe caloric restrictions and the increased release of insulin.

---

### DID YOU KNOW?

The body has no need for artificial sweeteners.

Artificial sweeteners are in the junk food group.

Purchasing soft drinks containing aspartame can become a consumer education lesson.

---

# BRAIN FOOD LESSONS

## Nutrition from the Rainforest

### An Elementary Lesson

## Focus Activity

Read *The Great Kapok Tree* (or any book you have about the rainforest) to the class and generate a discussion about the value of the rainforest.

After a brief discussion, ask the question, "What do popcorn, mangoes, salsa and cashews all have in common?" Sample several responses. They will make the connection that these foods all grow, or contain ingredients that are grown, in the rainforest. Ask students if they know in what part of the world we would likely find a rainforest. Bring out the globe. Ask any student to point out on the globe some countries that they think would contain rainforests. Ask them if they can think of any other foods that they suspect are grown in the rainforest. On the board or a large sheet of poster board generate a list of foods that are grow in the rainforest. This list should include, but not be limited to:

| | |
|---|---|
| Bananas | Pineapples |
| Oranges | Lemons |
| Coconuts | Cashews |
| Peppers | Ginger |
| Sugar | Cinnamon |
| Vanilla | Cocoa |
| Kola nut | Papaya |
| Mango. | |

Explain what "sustainably harvested" from the rainforest means (this will be printed on some food labels of certain rainforest snacks that boast of this accomplishment). This means that these foods came from the rainforest without harming the trees, plants, animals or people that live there. Eating these foods helps the rainforest, and they're good for you too! Discuss how we all need food to survive, and that making positive, nutritious rainforest-friendly choices about what we eat can help the rainforests survive as well.

## Activity

Have the students move into groups of three. This activity involves a group research project that may take two or three days.

Have each group choose a food that they enjoy eating and is grown in the rainforest. In the first part of the project, they are to research the nutritional value of the food. They can use any resources available to them. They are to write at least one paragraph on large newsprint about the nutritional value of the food, and illustrate the paragraph. For the second part of the assignment, they are to discover a few ways that we in the United States can help save the rainforest. Some websites to visit are:

Kids Corner: Rainforest Action Network at
http//www.ran org/ran/kids_action/index

KuKura, Guardian of the Rainforest at
http://greenKeepers.com

Amazonia Fun Quest at
http://www.amazoniafunquest.org

Save the Rainforest at
http://www.savetherainforest.org.

Using the web, along with other available resources, the teams of three will create a visual with ideas on how to save the rainforest. Words may be printed on the visuals as well. On day three, have each group present their two pieces of work.

## Reflection

Close the lesson with reflection questions such as:

What else did you learn about the rainforest during this task?

Why are the foods from the rainforest so healthful?

Will any of you be changing your eating habits because of this lesson?

# PEOPLE SEARCH: Nutrition

## A Middle School Activity

## Focus Activity

Ask the class if anyone knows what product in the grocery store is the largest seller?

Allow many answers to be discussed.

The item sold most often in the greatest volume relatively speaking is soft drinks.

## Activity: Introduce the People Search

FIND SOMEONE WHO:

1. Can verbalize a concern about his/her nutrition.

_____

2. Can predict what a grocery store will look like in the year 2025.

_____

3. Can explain what a phytochemical is, and list some of their benefits.

_____

4. Has the same junk food craving you do.

_____

5. Ate three servings of vegetables yesterday and can name them for you.

_____

6. Can compare and contrast our diet to our great grandparents diet.

_____

7. Can relate a situation where they reacted to some food in some way.

_____

8. Knows why fish is called "brain food".

_____

9. Can tell you what the hungriest organ in your body is.

_____

# PEOPLE SEARCH

## A High School Activity

## FIND SOMEONE WHO:

1. Can name ten green vegetables in 25 seconds.

_____

2. Can give you three good reasons why you should eat your vegetables.

_____

3. Can predict what shape their health will be in fifteen years from now.

_____

4. Can name three diet-related diseases people in the western world will die from.

_____

5. Can name a lean protein.

_____

6. Can explain what brain food does.

_____

7. Can compare and contrast the popular "Fast Foods" to the foods our grandparents ate.

_____

8. Will admit that "real men" eat vegetables.

_____

9. Cooks at home and will tell you what they prepared lately.

_____

# Chapter 5
## Not All Foods Are Good: Food Allergies

*"There are certain persons who cannot readily change their diet with impunity; and if they make any alterations in it for one day, even for a part of a day, are greatly injured thereby. Such persons, provided they take dinner when it is not their wont, immediately become heavy and inactive, both in body and mind ..."*

*– Hippocrates*

As early on as we can all remember, our parents, our teachers and our grandparents all recited the same mantra: "Drink your milk". Milk is just about as American as apple pie and the flag. To disagree with any authority on the subject of milk is simply un-American. In fact, it is sacrilegious! But many people are allergic or sensitive to milk. It is certain that you know someone who is lactose intolerant. Or perhaps you know someone whose doctor said not to give cows' milk to their infants after the child had been weaned.

That's because the milk they consumed during their childhood was different from the milk children consume today. Our grandparents drank milk that was delivered by a milk truck from the dairy farm. The milk came in bottles and the cream rose to the top of the bottle. It looked like a thick whipped cream on top, and that is exactly what it was. You shook the bottle to make the whole milk we know today. Milk, back then, was not homogenized.

The process of homogenization extends the shelf life of the milk. During this process, the fat in the milk is damaged. Homogenization breaks up the fat globules into extremely small droplets that are dispersed into the milk. Some of these fat particles can bypass digestive system and become absorbed directly into the bloodstream, carrying with them a destructive enzyme called xanthine oxidase (XO). As XO is carried through the bloodstream, it can damage the arteries by attacking plasmalogen, an integral part of the artery wall (Oster, in Gittleman, 1996) This fact alone should deter us from consuming so much milk. It does not however, and we still repeat the mantra our parents chanted to us, "drink your milk."

The subject of milk is still a touchy one in schools because milk is subsidized by the government, and schools usually encourage milk consumption. For some children this is fine; but for others who suffer from allergies or sensitivities to dairy products, one small carton of milk can ruin their day. Let's face it, Americans have a love affair with all of the dairy products that come from cows' milk. We love cheese, sour cream, cream cheese, cottage cheese, frozen yogurt, ice-cream, whip cream, milk shakes and milk chocolate. These lusty high-fat foods from the udder of the cow have come to be adored by most Americans.

The word allergy comes from two Greek words *allos* and *ergon* that mean other action. The body is doing something other than what it is supposed to do. As Dr. William Crook once said, "Allergies can't cause everything; but they can cause almost anything" (Crook, 2001). In the case of food, the body is supposed to be digesting it. If you have a true food allergy, well, that is not the case. Thus, a food allergy is an inability to digest, absorb and assimilate the nutrients from the food. Therefore, that food will travel through the bloodstream as an undigested food particle and deposit itself in the brain or in other body tissues, and wreak havoc wherever it lands.

This undigested food particle (allergen) is more dangerous than it sounds. The body perceives it as a foreign invader and thus sends out the troops to defend the body. The "troops" are the immune system. These food allergens are constantly bombarding the immune system and cause it to weaken over time. This is because fighting off the influx of allergic substances tire it out. As a consequence, the functions of the immune system slowly become more and more impaired and the child becomes prone to other diseases. The weakened immune system further impairs digestion. Progressive malnutrition begins. The brain suffers.

Most food allergies are delayed responses showing up one hour to three days after eating the allergic food. Since the reactions are delayed, most children keep eating the offending food to which they are allergic. Additionally, the delayed reaction involves a different antibody than the antibody doctors typically look for in allergies, thus even your child's physician may not fully understand

> Allergies are the body's immune system replying to perceived foreign elements.

what is occurring. Food allergy delayed reactions (which account for about 95% of food allergies) involves the immunoglobin G (IgG) instead of the immunoglobin E (IgE) which is the antibody known to be the culprit in airborne allergies such as those to pollen, dust and animal dander.

Allergies are the body's immune system replying to perceived foreign elements. One of the reasons that food allergies develop is because the food irritates the organs it comes into contact with. This causes a negative response. Another reason is because there is an inability in the digestive tract to properly assimilate the food. Thus, small food particles escape, undigested, and circulate into the blood stream where cells respond to them with uncomfortable effects (Zimmerman, 1999). Re-exposure to the same foods day in and day out impair the situation. The lining of the small intestine that the allergen comes into contact with has no time to repair itself from the irritation caused by the aggravating food. This is because kids usually consume the food to which they are allergic daily. Children are often picky eaters and only like a few foods, thus having limited food experience.

When you stop and think about the food you eat as an adult, you would probably come to the reach the realization that you eat the same foods, or at least the same food families, day in and day out. Within these food families, milk would most likely rank as a food eaten in some form everyday. There are three foods that most often cause allergies, including allergies affecting brain activity, and they are: wheat, milk and sugar. Unfortunately, these are the three most popular foods in America, especially with kids. Holidays and birthdays hold a triple threat – the trifecta! Cake usually contains all three allergens.

Since an allergy to food is an inability to digest, absorb, and assimilate that food, anyone can develop a food allergy at some stage of their life. Milk, being one of the common foods to which people are allergic and sensitive, carries a certain irony with it. And that is, milk is the very food we push on our children. The culprit in milk is casein. Casein is the protein in cows' milk, so it does not matter if the milk is 1%, 2% or skimmed, it will still contain casein. Dr. Leo Galland writes in his book *Superimmunity*, that for kids the most common allergen is milk (Galland, 1988).

The next culprit is wheat. White flour abounds in our food supply. Think of a day when you did not consume bread, pretzels, muffins, buns, cakes or cookies. All of these foods contain flour from wheat. The troubling part of wheat is the protein called gluten. Gluten is the very substance that makes wheat so perfect for baking, which is why wheat bread has a far smoother texture than rice bread.

Gluten, which is also found in other grains, destroys the small intestine's ability to absorb nutrients from food. Gluten, to a lesser degree is found in: rye, barley, oats, spelt, kamut and triticale. Spelt and kamut are in the wheat family; they are cousins to wheat. Triticale is a hybrid grain comprised of rye and wheat.

# Allergies and the Brain

Paradoxically, if a child suffers from a milk allergy due to the casein in the milk, or a wheat allergy from the gluten in wheat, dairy and wheat foods become impossible to resist. The allergic foods (especially milk, wheat and sugar) have a unique effect on the brain. As with drugs and alcohol, the first taste can lead to trouble. Soothing chemicals are released by the body to calm the irritation caused by the allergic reaction. Casein, the protein in cow's milk, stimulate the production of exorphins. Exorphins are opiate chemicals very similar to endorphins, which have a pleasurable effect. Over time, these pleasurable brain chemicals can become heavily addictive (Ross, 1999). So if a child who is allergic to milk does not get the milk "fix" he needs, he will not get the pleasurable feeling of comfort, which is so familiar. In this way, allergy is similar to addiction. In fact, going without the allergic food could land the child in an unbearable withdrawal state. You probably have had a similar experience trying to give up your morning cup of coffee. (Or, better yet, try removing all sugar from your diet and experience the difficulty and the feelings of withdrawal.)

> Allergy is similar to addiction.

The allergic response releases histamine in the brain, just like it does in other parts of the body, such as, the eyes, nose and lungs. The effect of histamine on the brain causes an increase of the escape of blood serum into the surrounding brain tissues. This causes a waterlogged effect and, as a result, memory and attention are decreased (Zimmerman, 1999). Brain fatigue sets in. This is why an innocent carton of milk for an allergic child could literally ruin their day.

Allergies that impair brain function but show little evidence elsewhere in the body were first termed hidden allergies by William Philpott, M.D., and Dwight Kalita, PhD, in 1984. Today, they are sometimes referred to as hidden or delayed reactions. In 1980 in his seminal book, *Allergies Your Hidden Enemy*, Dr. Theron G. Randolph wrote of hidden food addictions. He states:

"Allergies to commonly eaten food are not so readily detected or avoided, however. Let us say, for instance, that you develop an allergy to milk early in life. At first, this may have resulted in an acute reaction such as a rash or a cough. In time, if the allergy was not recognized and controlled, the symptoms may have become more generalized and less easily detected. Since you probably went on drinking milk or eating milk products almost every day, one day's symptoms blurred into the next day's. You developed a chronic disease, such as arthritis, migraine or depression. It never occurred to you that your daily dose of milk was the source of the problem" (Randolph and Moss, 1980, p. 16).

> Allergies to commonly eaten food are not so readily detected.

The Food Allergy Network, along with others, estimates that nearly 50% of Americans suffer from food intolerance and sensitivities. Whether the child is allergic (reaction is more pronounced) or intolerant (the reaction may be delayed and more subtle) milk, wheat and sugar are on the list of common culprits (Fenster, 1999).

Some of the emotional and cognitive symptoms a child with food allergies can exhibit are Jekyll and Hyde behaviors – irritability, inability to concentrate, mental fatigue, depression, anxiety, crying jags, mood swings, confusion, forgetfulness, abrupt personality change, hyperactivity, and some phobias. If any of these symptoms occur continuously after eating or drinking some food, determine and record what your child ate or drank.

Some of the more common symptoms are: headache, diarrhea, eczema, acne, ear infections, gas, bloating, stomach ache, dark circles under the eyes, eczema, runny nose, sneezing, postnasal drip, excessive phlegm, nausea and vomiting.

# What Can You Do?

As a teacher or parent, begin by removing the food or foods the child eats most often. Usually, but not always, the offending food falls into the common allergen group of milk, wheat, sugar, corn, eggs, peanuts, citrus, soy and chocolate. Begin by removing the food the child eats every day. A good place to begin is with milk and milk products. Remove all cheese, butter, ice-cream, sour cream, cottage cheese and salad dressings containing milk. This may seem difficult, but it can be accomplished.

Find a nice natural food market and pick out some almond milk, rice milk, and cheeses if they have them. There are even ice-cream

Learn to read labels.

alternatives that kids really enjoy. Learn to read labels. If the effort seems daunting at first, just know that the rewards are well worth it when your student or child feels and learns better. The results will convince you.

**BRAIN JOGGER**

Have the students sit in groups of three and have one student act as the recorder. Challenge them to think back two or three days and to record all of the foods they have eaten in those days. Record. Now classify the foods into the three food groups. Additionally, classify the foods into the groups of common allergens. Which foods contain sugar, milk, wheat flour, peanuts or chocolate? Discuss as a class.

# BRAIN FOOD LESSONS

## Living Foods

### An Elementary Lesson

## Focus Activity

Ask the children what happens to fruits that are left out on the counter for a long time. What do they see? What happens to the fruit? Have them name some foods that they have seen begin to rot with mould, and get rather soft. Ask them to conjecture about what happened to the mouldy fruit.

Explain that live foods are perishable! Use the word perishable as a vocabulary or spelling word of the week, and talk about what it means.

Have a discussion about how plant foods in their raw state are alive!

## Activity

Divide the children into five working groups. Bring in: garbanzo beans (chick peas); green lentils; black beans; black-eyed peas; and raw, unsalted sunflower seeds. Give each group a large jar and have the students soak the seeds overnight. The next day, empty the soaking water, place a cloth over the mouth of the jar and poke a few holes in it for air, and place the jar in a dark place in the classroom overnight. The next day, most of the peas and beans will begin to sprout. The garbanzo beans will take the longest time to sprout; they may need another day. Taste the sprouts. Make a salad dressing for them. Have the children rate the sprouts.

## Reflection

Talk about what happened to the beans. They were stone hard in the beginning. Now they have softened and some of them have tails! How did this occur?

# Link and Think

## A Middle School Lesson

## Focus Activity

Have the students write down on a piece of paper what they ate yesterday. Do not have them sign the piece of paper. Write the following categories on the board to prompt their thinking: Breakfast, Lunch, Tea, Snacks, Beverages. Some of them may have trouble remembering. Collect all papers.

Have three students come to the board and tally all of the entries into the three food groups of: Plant Foods, Animal Foods or Junk Foods.

Discuss the results.

## Activity:

Do the same thing the very next day. Compare and contrast the two days.

## Reflection:

Have the students reflect in their journals on what they discovered about their own eating habits.

# My Food, My Mood

## A High School Lesson

## Focus Activity

Ask the students if they have ever eaten anything when they were not hungry. Have them share. What foods did they choose in this non-hungry state? What made them eat when they were not hungry?

## Activity

Have the students keep a food journal for two days (that is enough time). Have them notice how they felt with each food encounter. Were they truly hungry? What foods did they eat? What foods called out to them? What did they notice about their moods before and after each food encounter?

## Reflection

Ask the students to share what they learned from this experience.

*"A healthy body is necessary for a healthy brain"*
*– Plato, 400 BC*

Circulation. Oxygen. New neuronal pathways. Enhancement of neuronal metabolism, and stress reduction. These are but a few of the good reasons to promote movement, activity, physical education and extra-curricular sports events in schools. Throughout history, it has been generally acknowledged that exercise benefits the mind. Thomas Jefferson noted that, "No less than two hours a day should be devoted to exercise." When President John F. Kennedy established his physical goals for America's children he responded to Jefferson's view by saying, "If the man who wrote the Declaration of Independence, was Secretary of State, and twice president, could give it two hours, our children can give it ten minutes."

Specifically, what does exercise do for the hungry brain?

1. enhances neuronal metabolism

2. supplies the brain with nerve growth factor

3. reduces stress.

# Enhancement of Neuronal Metabolism

One of the most wide-reaching effects of exercise on the brain is neuronal metabolism. What that means is there is an improvement in the total energy exchange between the brain cells and the outside environment. This energy exchange includes the exchange of oxygen, nutrients, and cellular waste products. These three functions of neuronal metabolism are improved considerably by exercise because exercise improves blood circulation to the brain.

Exercise increases the amount of oxygen and glucose that the brain receives. It tones some of the neurotransmitters such as norepinephrine and dopamine. It increases the availability of brain-related enzymes such as coenzyme Q-10. It increases output of some neuropeptides, including endorphins. It decreases high-density lipoprotein, which clogs brain circulation. It lowers blood pressure. And it helps stabilize blood sugar levels, thereby assisting in the stabilizing of mood and energy.

> Exercise increases the amount of oxygen and glucose that the brain receives.

# Nerve Growth Factor and Brain-Derived Neurotropic Factor

Exercise has been proven to produce abundant amounts of nerve growth factor (NGF), and everyone can produce nerve growth factor, everyday! Just by exercising. Nerve growth factor is a hormone. Some theorists believe that the nerve growth factor is the reason for Alzheimer's Disease. The reasoning is this; brain cells die because they so not receive proper amounts of nerve growth factor. Nerve growth factor stimulates regeneration of the brain. One of the greatest benefits exercise has on NGF is in the area of the brain that is the most plastic, the hippocampus, which is the brain's primary memory center. This regional concentration accounts for much of the improvement in memory experienced by elderly people who begin to exercise. NGF however, also supports neurons throughout the brain.

Nerve growth factor and another similar hormone, brain-derived neurotropic factor, or BDNF, increase the production of the important neurotransmitters acetylcholine and dopamine, and increase the number of dopamine receptors. Moreover, BDNF and NGF increase the activity of neuronal free-radical scavengers that protect brain cells.

In the 1990s scientists at the University of California at Irvine were thrilled by experiments showing that putting rats on treadmills induced the brain cells to produce a chemical "growth factor" that spurs growth of dendrites by expanding their communication networks. What was most remarkable to them was that the neuronal growth happened not only in parts of the brain that control motoric movement, but also in areas that control reasoning, thinking, learning and memory. The same researchers found that older individuals who exercised scored better on tests of cognitive function than those individuals who did not exercise.

## Stress Reduction

Exercise has more benefits to consider. All of the above mentioned effects help to reduce the stress response. Reduction of stress equals clearer thinking. Additionally, exercise reduces stress by helping to decrease depression, and the output of cortisol by placing a "brake" on the stress response.

The impact of physical activity also includes elevated serotonin and endorphin signaling. This means possible mood improvement, enhanced self-esteem, and a true sense of wellbeing, along with reduced feelings of pain.

> Reduction of stress equals clearer thinking.

Unfortunately, stress decreases BDNF, because stress produced cortisol destroys BDNF. However exercise can help to restore the BDNF that cortisol destroys. Additionally, exercising will help reduce chronic cortisol oversecretion.

Another effect of exercise is that it releases endorphins. These "feel good" neuropeptides are the body's own opiates. They begin to be produced in abundant quantities after about fifteen to thirty minutes of exercise. After they are secreted, they remain active for about five hours; almost as long as a school day!

A good brain food rule is, "What's good for the heart is good for the head."

It is vitally important to understand that brain health means good circulation. One way to optimize circulation is through movement. Age-associated memory problems are often exacerbated by poor circulation. Neurons killed by cortisol and other negative factors almost always impede blood flow to healthy neurons, increasing memory loss and concentration problems. Additionally, vascular plaque caused by excessive dietary fat contributes to decreased blood flow to brain cells. The brain is critically dependent upon abundant blood flow, because it requires about 25% of all blood pumped by the heart. Therefore, any disruption of cerebral circulation has a profoundly negative effect upon the brain. A good brain food rule is, "What's good for the heart is good for the head."

Today, only thirty percent of all children from first grade through high school get even thirty minutes of exercise daily at school.

Another reason to exercise is that being overweight is not good for the brain. It can foster insulin resistance, high blood pressure and possible diabetes, that can lead to impaired memory and subtle damage to brain cells.

When you think about it, engaging in a two-hour daily workout, as Jefferson recommended, was more than commonplace; for our very recent ancestors it was every day of their lives. As a matter of course, they expended in their daily jobs as much energy as we would if we walked a twenty-six mile marathon every day.

In the 1920s, the shift into industrialization had begun to radically decrease the level of physical activity in the United States and other Western nations. It was around this time that the cardiovascular "epidemic" began. Furthermore, by the 1960s physical activity had declined markedly. Today, only thirty percent of all children from first grade through high school get even thirty minutes of exercise daily at school.

So perhaps the pejorative attitude toward the "dumb jocks" looking like they just busted out of San Quentin may be the smartest thing we discard for the sake of the brain.

## BRAIN JOGGER

Talk to the physical education teacher and see if she will come to your class for a stretch break. She can model some safe stretches to use in the classroom. Ask her to teach some partner stretches to add more fun.

Bring in a Yoga or Pilates tape to study some of the "moves" to teach the class.

Just get up and walk around with an activity related to your content: a People Search; a Carousel around the room; a spelling or math drill standing up; playing catch for questions answered.

Orchestrate a jump rope competition to encourage this "forgotten favorite" exercise. Jumping rope is ther perfect exercise to "jump-start" the brain. It yields all the benefits of rigorous exercise. Jumping rope improves the total energy between the body and the environment; it reduces the stress in the body, which translates into clearer thinking. Jump ropes address the nutrition/cognition connection of fitness and wellness programs in today's schools.

■ □ ■ □ ■

# BRAIN FOOD LESSONS

## Match and Mirror

### An Elementary Lesson

## Focus Activity

Have the children move around the room with some music on. Stop the music and have the students "freeze".

## Activity

Have the children find a partner and ask them to stand face-to-face.

Now have one partner take the lead and do some movements facing the other person. This should be done standing close, but in their own space. Now, simultaneously, the non-lead partner matches and mirrors the lead person. Do this for about 45 seconds. Reverse roles.

## Reflection

Ask the students to share what they liked or did not like about the activity. Ask them which role they preferred.

# Movement Read

## A Middle School Lesson

## Focus Activity

Have the students read a passage from one of their favorite novels. Give them a few minutes of silent reading time and then tell them to stop.

## Activity

Now have them stand in a circle holding their books. Have them read silently for the same amount of minutes as above while they are walking in the circle.

## Reflection

How did they feel while walking? Was it difficult or was it easier? Discuss.

# A Brain Stretch

## A High School Lesson

## Focus Activity

Have the students read the same passage silently, for four minutes.

## Activity

Have the students get up and literally stretch for another four minutes. After the stretch, have them sit down and re-read the passage for four minutes again.

## Reflection

What did they notice?

## Snacks For Kids

### Kangaroo Pita Pockets

1 large pita pocket
1 mini pita pocket

fresh cut (diced):
celery
carrots
pickles
peppers
lettuce
cheese
tuna salad
chicken salad
peanut butter
bananas
almond butter
raisins.

Let your child stuff the large pita with whatever filling they desire. Stuff the smaller pita as well. Place them on a plate together in a kangaroo shape. First the larger pita and then the smaller one as a head. The pita is a "pocket bread". The kangaroo is a marsupial, which means they have a pouch or a pocket in which to carry their babies.

Make a tail with a yellow pepper strip and ears with raisins.

■ □ ■ □ ■

# Monkey Business

Slice two large sweet potatoes into 1/4-inch rings.

Take the sweet potato rings and steam them in a double boiler, bamboo steamer, or metal steamer that sits on top of a saucepan. Or microwave them in a little water for about 5–7minutes until they are soft. Keep the skins on.

Place the rings on a plate for kids to decorate. As toppings you can use:

Raisins
Cinnamon
Chopped nuts
Bananas
Peaches
Jam
Plum baby food
Applesauce
Granola
Corn flakes and mashed bananas
Peanut butter.

I have a special topping I like to make to have the kids spread around their sweet potato rings.

About 2–3 tablespoons of soy margarine (Spectrum or any other non-hydrogenated kind); you can also use butter
1 teaspoon of vanilla
1 teaspoon pure maple syrup from the tree (health food store item)
1 teaspoon freshly ground cinnamon.

Melt the butter or margarine in a small saucepan and slowly add the rest of the ingredients. Spread this tasty sauce with a spatula onto the sweet potato rings. Place the rings on a plate in the shape of a monkey. Monkeys love to eat sweet potatoes. They eat them raw. Sweet potatoes are one of the

most nutritious foods that grow beneath the ground. They
are filled with carotenoid antioxidants and they also contain
calcium. They are high in vitamins A and C, with a fair
amount of thiamine. All plant foods contain fiber.

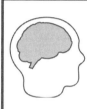

## MORE BRAIN JOGGERS

Have the students represent the following
terms visually. They can make little
colored cards and quiz each other.
Each term should have a separate card.
The terms are humorous and relate to a
nutritious food.

## BROCCOPHOBIA

Many children suffer from this. It's the fear of ingesting too
many anti-cancer properties. (Broccoli has at least 33.)

## EMPTY NOSHER

A person who noshes on junk food to the exclusion of more
nutritious foods.

## A NO-BRAINER

Someone who never eats: cold water fish, walnuts, and
flax seeds. These foods are high in Omega-3 essential fatty
acids, which are good for the brain.

## ULCER EATER

Someone who believes that drinking milk will cure ulcers.
This person should eat bananas, plantains, cabbage
juice, and surprise surprise – hot peppers, which contain
capsaicin that protects, by stimulating nerves in the stomach
wall, dilating blood vessels and improving blood flow.

■ □ ■ □ ■

### CORNY JOKE

This is the rumor that has been circulated, that corn is a vegetable. It's a grain and has 37 anti-cancer properties.

### A COOL DUDE

A male who eats cucumbers. Cucumbers are 10 degrees cooler than the air around them, and contain about 15 anti-cancer properties.

### THE NIGHT STALKER

Someone who raids the refrigerator in the evening for celery, which contains at least 27 anti-cancer agents, and can lower their blood pressure.

### NOT THE MARRYING KIND

These are two people who "can't e lope." Cantaloupe has at least 12 anti-cancer compounds.

### RAY'S SINS

A person named Ray, who steals grapes, dries them, and then covers them with chocolate. Grapes and raisins have at least 24 anti-cancer properties.

### MELLOW YELLOW

A person who becomes peaceful after eating bananas for their gastrointestinal benefits, and for the 11 cancer-fighting properties.

### PEA POSTEROUS PERSON

Someone who thinks they can skip eating their peas. Peas contain 19 cancer-preventative agents and high amounts of soluble fiber that lowers cholesterol.

■ □ ■ □ ■

ANTI-VAMP

A person who chews raw garlic to ward off colds, and to infuse their body with 35 cancer-preventative compounds.

BEANEVOLENT

The act of treating beans kindly. Beans are high in soluble fiber, which lowers blood cholesterol; they also contain cancer-fighting compounds, help lower blood pressure and are a great source of plant protein.

**MORE BRAIN JOGGERS**

Have the students do the same thing they did for the humorous word. Each student can create a card with a visual representation of the term. Then they teach each other the terms using their own card.

# Nutrition Terms

NUTRIENTS

The human body requires energy to perform its voluntary and involuntary activities. This energy is provided by nutrients in the food we eat. The nutrients that the body can synthesize itself are nonessential nutrients. Others, termed essential nutrients, must be obtained from the food we ingest.

MACRONUTRIENTS

The macronutrients are water, fiber, protein, carbohydrates and fats. With the exception of fiber, all of these macronutrients are necessary for the brain.

## MICRONUTRIENTS

The micronutrients are minerals, vitamins, and phytochemicals.

## PHYTOCHEMICALS

Plant chemicals are the general name for more specific nutrients. There are many phytochemicals, and more and more are being discovered. They have names such as: carotinoids, quercitin, indole-3-carbinol, phenylisothiocyanate, glucosinolates, bioiflavonoids, polyphenols, and others. Phytochemicals are recently discovered in the world of nutrition, yet they are the subject of a lot of research, especially in the area of cancer prevention. These phytochemicals are loved by the brain. They keep the brain young. Fruits, vegetables, nuts, seeds, sprouts and whole grains contain these phytochemicals. The deeper the color of the plant, the greater the amount of the phytochemical.

## FIBER

Fiber is a substance found only in plants. Fiber, now considered a macronutrient, is a non-digestible form of a mucopolysaccheride. Scientists have discovered two main types of fiber important for proper human functioning – soluble and insoluble fiber. Soluble fiber is found in fruits, and grains such as oats and barley. Soluble fiber has been found to lower blood cholesterol. Insoluble fiber, found in some grains and vegetables, can help prevent colon cancer. People, who are low on fiber intake will most likely suffer from a variety of health challenges in the long term. Lack of enough fibers can cause haemorrhoids, varicose veins, diverticulitus and constipation.

## BOWEL TRANSIT TIME

The time it takes for food to move through the intestinal tract from mouth to bowel movement. Fiber helps to increase the rate of bowel transit time. In countries where people consume a large amount of fruit and vegetables, the bowel transit time is about 24 hours. In the United States, however, the average bowel transit time is 72 hours. A long bowel transit time is undesirable in terms of good health. Without fiber, bowel transit time is slowed down to an unhealthy rate.

FOOD ALLERGY

An inability of the digestive tract to digest, absorb and properly assimilate certain food or foods, causing an array of health problems. Any food can become a potential allergen, and any individual can become allergic to any food. The five most common foods to which people are allergic are corn, milk, wheat, sugar and eggs.

HYPOGLYCEMIA

A condition of low blood sugar. Glucose, the primary fuel for the brain and for the muscles, is not available, due to poor diet, skipping meals, and insulin sensitivity.

COMPLEX CARBOHYDRATES

Complex carbohydrates contain more starch than sugar, usually with the fiber intact.

SIMPLE CARBOHYDRATES

Simple carbohydrates usually come in the form of sugars.

OMEGA-3 ESSENTIAL FATTY ACIDS

Omega-3 essential fatty acids are very important fats that the body needs for brain functioning, wound healing, nerve endings, skin care and hair care. These special fats are found in fatty ocean fish, fish oils, walnuts, kale, purslane, and flax seeds. Omega-3 is essential for the brain. It must be eaten.

# Glossary of Terms

**Acetylcholine**
A neurotransmitter used by the nervous system, it is synthesized from a substance found commonly in foods, called choline. It is thought to play a role in memory.

**Alkaloid**
Any of a group of organic compounds that have a drug-like activity, as found in tobacco.

**Allicin**
Predominant phytochemical in garlic, the major organic compound sulfur compound contributing to garlic odor.

**Alliums**
A family of vegetables that includes garlic, onions, leeks and chives; known for contribution of the phytochemical allicin and related sulfur compounds.

**Alpha carotenoids**
Key carotenoids found primarily in pumpkin, carrots, cantaloupe, guava and yellow corn.

**Amino acid**
A group of compounds that make up the building blocks of proteins. Humans use approximately 22 different types of amino acids.

**Antibody**
A protein produced by the immune system from "B cells" or bone marrow-derived cells.

**Antigen**
A molecule recognized as foreign by the immune system.

**Antioxidant**
These are compounds that render free radicals harmless. They may be minerals, vitamins, enzymes or phytochemicals. Common examples include Vitamin E, beta-carotene, and Vitamin C.

### Artificial flavors
Artificial flavors can come from purely synthetic or natural sources. Most food manufacturers do not list the exact ingredients of artificial flavors, which may consist of allergy-provoking substances. They can be irritating to the brain and nervous system.

### Axons
An extension of the nerve cell that carries the signal away from the nerve cell body to ultimately connect with another nerve cell or a cell of a different type.

### Azodicarbonamide (ADA)
ADA is a conditioner used to bleach and mellow the flavor of white flour used commercially in foods. The allergic reactions to azodicarbonamide include asthma, coughs, wheezing and rashes.

### B Cell
Immune cell producing antibodies, located in the bone marrow.

### Brain Compatible
Teaching and learning processes that parallel or compliment the way the brain learns.

### Brain stem
One of the three major parts of the brain, it receives sensory input and monitors vital functions such as heartbeat, body temperature and digestion.

### Butylated hydroxyanisole (BHA)
This antioxidant preservative is used in food and beverages to prevent oxidation and retard rancidity in fats, oils and oil-containing foods. A synthetic chemical, BHA can cause allergic reaction, and in laboratory studies has been found to be weakly estrogenic in vitro. Dose-dependent European studies indicate a high incidence of cancerous and benign tumors in laboratory animals fed BHA. BHA is labeled as a possible carcinogen by the World Health Organization. Not recommended for the hungry delicate brain.

### Butlated Hydroxytoluene (BHT)
BHT is a prohibited food additive in England. Like BHA, BHT retards rancidity in foods such as cereals, potato chips, candies, oils, shortenings, frozen pork sausage and many others. It may alter behavior and provoke hyperactivity in children. Published findings indicate BHT induces tumors in laboratory animals.

■ ☐ ■ ☐ ■

## Casein
Casein is the principal protein in cow's milk and is used as a texturizer in ice-cream, ice milk, fruit sherbets, frozen custard, coffee creamer, water-packed tuna, and many other foods. Casein may appear as sodium or calcium caseinate on labels, and is the protein to which milk-allergic individuals are most likely reactive. Milk allergic individuals should avoid all products containing casein.

## Central nervous system
The brain and spinal cord are considered the central nervous system. Nerves that run outside of the skull and spinal column are known as the peripheral nervous system.

## Cholesterol
A sterol found in the diet in animal fats, cholesterol is a vital component of the body's biochemistry used to form steroid hormones such as estrogen, testosterone and cortisone. The human body makes about 3,000 mg of cholesterol daily – roughly the equivalent of one dozen eggs. Roughly one-quarter of the lipids (fatty substances) in myelin occur as cholesterol.

## Choline
A nutritional substance the brain uses to manufacture the neurotransmitter acetylcholine. Choline is sometimes used as a supplement to enhance mental function.

## Dendrite
An extension of the nerve cell that receives an impulse and carries it back to the nerve cell body.

## Dendritic branches
Like the branches of a tree, they project off the main dendrite. Increased branching allows for greater communication between nerve cells.

## Dendritic spines
Tiny structures that project off the dendrite or dendritic branch. They increase the number of synaptic connections that each neuron can make with other neurons. This increases the efficiency with which various regions of the body communicate with one another. There can be literally thousands of dendritic spines allowing for up to 20,000 synapses with other nerve cells.

### Dextrose
Dextrose, or corn sugar, is used as a coloring agent and sweetener in numerous prepared foods such as cookies, breads and highly processed foods. Dextrose is a simple sugar with the same chemical composition as glucose.

### DHA (docosahexaenoic acid)
A long-chain polyunsaturated fatty acid derived from dietary alpha-linolenic acid. AHA is also found in foods such as salmon, herring, sardines, tuna and mackerel. It contains twenty-two carbons, six double bonds, and is an omega-3 fatty acid. This is written 22:6n-3. DHA is the most-important Omega-3 fatty acid found in the brain and is highly concentrated in the retina.

### EPA (eicosapentaenoic acid)
A long-chain polyunsaturated fatty acid derived from dietary alpha-linolenic acid. It contains 20 carbons, five double bonds, and is an Omega-3 fatty acid. EPA can be made into PGE3, an anti-inflammatory substance that helps counter the effects of the inflammatory PGE2 substances. EPA is not found in the brain, but can be converted into DHA for use in the brain. EPA is important in the brain's blood supply.

### Enzymes
Proteins induce changes in biochemical systems. Practically, they assist in changing one substance into something else. For example, delta-6-desaturase helps to add double bonds into fatty acid molecules making them more unsaturated. It converts alpha-linolenic acid to EPA. Another enzyme then converts EPA into the brain-fat DHA. Enzymes usually require vitamins and minerals as cofactors and catalysts.

### Free radical
A highly reactive molecule, atom or molecular fragment that has a free or unpaired electron, free radicals react quickly with protein, fat, and carbohydrate in the body. They are also capable of reacting with almost any cell or tissue causing damage. Free radicals are essential to the function of the human body. Problems occur when free-radical production begins to exceed the body's ability to protect against them. This occurs in many disease processes. Antioxidants protect against free radicals. The highly unsaturated fatty acids in the brain are especially sensitive to free radicals.

■ □ ■ □ ■

## Gluten

Gluten is the protein portion of the grain. Grains containing gluten include wheat, rye, barley and oats. Gluten is the substance in these grains that causes the allergic reaction in people who are allergic to wheat. The most severe form of gluten intolerance is called celiac disease. It used to be thought that gluten intolerance was rare. But recent findings show that more and more people are unable to assimilate wheat and similar grains because of excessive consumption of these foods.

## Glycemic index

The potential of a sugar or carbohydrate to raise blood sugar levels; high glycemic index foods tend to raise insulin levels higher. High insulin may stimulate the conversion of Omega-6 fatty acids into the inflammatory arachidonic acid.

## Lipid

A general term used to describe fatty molecules derived from the diet. Fatty acids, triglycerides, phospholipids, and waxes are included in this group. Cholesterol is technically not a fat, but a sterol. However, it is still considered a lipid.

## Monounsaturated fat

An unsaturated fatty acid that contains one double bond.

## Nerve

A cell that carries information to and from the central nervous system.

## Neural fat

Fats important to the structure and function of the nervous system.

## Neurotransmitter

A substance, often a protein or amino acid, which facilitates communication between cells in the nervous system. They affect such things as mood, behavior, memory, thirst, hunger, sleep, muscle contraction, and other processes, especially thinking. In the receptor interaction, the neurotransmitter is like the ship that must fit into the specifically-shaped dock.

## Norepinephrine

A neurotransmitter involved in alertness, concentration and aggression.

### Receptors
Sites on the surface of cells where hormones, neurotransmitters and other substances can attach. Receptors can be likened to a dock into which a ship of a very specific shape must fit. They are of specific size and shape necessary to react very specifically to another molecule. When a molecule attaches to a receptor the nerve signal can be sent. Receptors are strongly influenced by the fatty-acid structure of the cell membrane.

### Synapse
The gap between nerve cells. It is the point where the bulb-shaped tip of one neuron abuts the bulb, shaft or spine of another neuron. A tiny gap exists between them, which allows for the flow of neurotransmitters and other substances. The synaptic membranes of the neuron are highly concentrated with DHA. DHA deficiency adversely affects function of the synapse. The synapse is critical to all nerve cell communication.

### Trans fatty acid
An unsaturated fatty acid that has been altered in a way that causes a flip-flop at the position of the double bond. This changes the fatty acid from its normal curved shape to an arrow shape. These harmful fats are more likely to be solid at body temperature. In animal studies, they have been shown to change cell membrane fluidity and have been found to enter the brain. These undesirable fats should be avoided.

# Resources

**For Biochemical Balancing Treatment (mild, moderate, and severe)**
The Pfeiffer Treatment Center
4575 Weaver Parkway,
Warrenville, Illinois 600555
Phone (630) 505-0300
Fax (630) 836-0667
www.HRIPTC.org

The Pfeiffer Treatment Center is a nonprofit medical research and treatment facility; a branch of Health Research Institute (HRI). Since the opening of the center in 1989, it has treated more that 12,000 patients who suffer from: behavioral dysfunctions, depression, learning disabilities, bipolar disorder, autism, schizophrenia and anxiety, by balancing body and brain chemistry. The on-site HRI pharmacy compounds nutrients, hormones and other biochemical's to reduce the number of pills in a prescription using special customized methods. Their newest program is on the natural, clinical approach to the biochemical aspects of life-cycle changes of both men and women, such as aging, menopause and puberty. This is a day clinic staffed by a team of physicians, chemists, and other professionals specializing in the effects of biochemistry on behavior, thought and mood.

**Individual Health Solutions**
8323 Sharon Drive
Frederick, Maryland 20704
Phone (301) 874-1797
Fax (301) 874-1798
www.IndividualHealthsolutions.com

Individual Health Solutions is an on-line order source for specific vitamin and mineral compounds using the balancing solutions based on the work of doctors Pfeiffer and Walsh. These solution products are more appropriate for people with mild to moderate symptoms of depression, anxiety, seasonal allergies, food allergies, glucose dysregualtion, digestive problems, weight gain or weight loss.

### Organic Foods

Your best source of organic foods is your local farmer or nearby organic farm stand. Growing your own food is also a great idea, if you have a good growing season and some time. If not, there are the local health food stores like Whole Foods, Wild Oats, and local independent natural food stores.

### Dairy-free and wheat-free food sources:

### Imagine Foods

Makers of Rice Dream Products. Non-dairy beverages and frozen desserts as well as soups, veggie burgers and more. Grocery store available.

### Aunt Candice Foods

Gluten and casein-free.
www.auntcandicefoods.com

### Gluten solutions

For mail-order dairy-free and wheat-free foods.
Shipped right to your door.
www.glutensolutions.com

### Trufree

Sell a range of wheat, gluten, milk and egg-free products for people who have an adverse reaction to food. Also provides recipes.
www.trufree.co.uk

### Dairy Free Health food Store

Hundreds of products for a healthy, dairy-free diet.
www.shopbydiet.com

### Vance's Foods ™

Vance's Darifree is a fat-free milk alternative that was developed to be free of protein for the many individuals on a protein-restricted diet.
www.vancefoods.com

# References

Appleton, N. (1988). *Lick the Sugar Habit.* Garden City Park, NY: Avery Publishing.

Astrand, P. O. (1992). Physical activity and fitness. *American Journal of Clinical Nutrition, 55:* 1231–1236.

Atkins, R. (2000). *Dr. Atkins' Age-Defying Diet Revolution.* New York: St Martins Press.

Bang, H. O. and Dyerberg, J. (1978). Eicosapentaenoic acid and the prevention of thrombosis and atherosclerosis, *Lancet,* 2(8081): 117–119.

Barnard, N. (2001). *Turn Off the Fat Genes.* New York: Harmony Books.

Barrett, S. (1992). *It's All in Our Head: A Guide to Understanding your Brain and Boosting your Brain Power.* Minneapolis, MN: Free Spirit Publishing.

Belury, M. A. (1995). *Nutrition Reviews, 53*(4): 83–89.

Benton, D. and Haller, J. (1995). The impact of long-term vitamin supplementation on cognitive functioning. *Psychopharmacology,* 117: 298–305.

Bernstein, A. (1990). Vitamin B6 in clinical neurology. *Annals of the New York Academy of Sciences, 585:* 250–60.

Beutler, E. (1989). Nutritional and metabolic aspects of glutathione. *Annual Review of Nutrition, 9:* 287–302.

Bland, J. (1996). *The Twenty Day Rejuvenation Diet Program.* New Canaan, CT: Keats Publishing.

Bland, J. (1999). *Genetic Nutritioneering: How You Can Modify Inherited Traits and Live a Longer, Healthier Life.* Los Angeles, Keats Publishing.

Blaylock, R. L. (1997). *Excitotoxins: The Taste That Kills.* Santa Fe, NM: Health Press.

Block, M. A. (1996). *No More Ritalin: Treating ADHD Without Drugs.* New York: Kensington Books.

Carper, J. (1993) *Food: Your Miracle Medicine.* New York: Harper Collins.

Carper, J. (2001). *Your Miracle Brain.* New York: Harper Collins.

Cherkin, A. (1987). Interaction of nutritional factors with memory processing, pp 70–91 In Essman, W. B. (1987). *Nutrients and Brain Function.* Basel, Switzerland: Karger.

Conners, B. (1989) *Feeding the Brain: How Foods Affect Children.* New York: Plenum Press.

Crook, W. (1991). *Help for the Hyperactive Child.* Jackson, TN: Professional Books.

Crook, W. (2001). Personal communication.

De Wardener, H. E. and Lennox, B. (1947) Cerebral beriberi (Wernicke's encephalopathy). Review of 52 cases in a Singapore prisoner-of-war hospital. *Lancet* 1: 11–17.

DesMaisons, K. (1999). *Potatoes not Prozac.* New York: Simon and Schuster.

Diamond, M. and Hopson J. (1998). *Magic Trees of the Mind: How to Nurture your Child's Intelligence, Creativity, and Healthy Emotions from Birth Through Adolescence.* New York: Plume.

Edelman, E. (1996). *Natural Healing of Schizophrenia.* Eugene, Oregon: Borage Books.

Erasmus, U. (1986). *Fats and Oils.* Vancouver, Canada: Alive Publishing.

Fallon, S. (1995). *Nourishing Traditions.* San Diego, CA: Promotion Publishing.

Felix, C. (1991). All that we can be. *The Felix Letter: A Commentary on Nutrition,* 58: 1–4.

Fenster, C. (1999). *Special Diet Celebrations.* Littleton, CO: Savory Palate Inc.

Galland, L. (1988). *Superimmunity for Kids.* New York: Copestone Press.

Girardi, N. L., Shaywitz, S. E., Shaywitz, B. A., Marchione, K., Fleischman, S. J., Jones, T. W. and Tamborlane, W. V. (1995). Blunted catecholamine responses after glucose ingestion in children with attention deficit disorder. *Journal of Pediatric Research*, 38(4): 539–542.

Gittleman, A. L. (1996). *Beyond Pritikin*. Bantam Books.

Gittleman, A. L. (2002). *The Fat Flush Plan*. New York: McGraw-Hill.

Giuffre, G., Barresi, G., Vitarelli, E., Grosso, M. and Tuccari, G. (1999). Simple Mucin-type carbohydrate antigens in Helicobacter pylori-positive chronic active gastritis. *Virchows Archiv.*, 435(4) 458–460.

Gormley, J. (2000). What's the Big Fat Deal? *Better Nutrition*, 12(62): 68–69.

Hausman, P. (1981). *Jack Sprat's Legacy*. Richard Marek Publishers.

Heaney, R. (1982). Calcium nutrition and bone health in the elderly. *American Journal of Clinical Nutrition*, 36: 986.

Hoffer, A. (1957). Treatment of schizophrenia with nicotinic acid and nicotinamide. *Journal of Clinical and Experimental Psychopathology*, 18: 131–58.

Jacobson, M. and Maxwell, B. (1994). *What Are We Feeding Our Kids?* New York: Workman Press.

Jones, T. W., Tamborlane, W. V., Borg, W. P., Boulware, S. D., McCarthy, G. and Sherwin, R. S. (1995). Enhanced adrenomedullary response and increased susceptibility to neuroglycopnea: Mechanisms underlying the effects of sugar ingestion in healthy children. *Journal of Pediatrics*, 126(2): 171–177.

Khalsa, D. S. and Stauth, C. (1997). *Brain Longevity: The Breakthrough Medical Program That Improves your Mind and Memory*. New York: Warner Books.

Klaper, M. (1987). *Vegan Nutrition*. Umatilla, FL: Gentle World Inc.

Knittel, L. (2001). Heading off heart disease. *Delicious Living Magazine Annual Guide, August 2001*.

Krohn, J. (1991). *Whole Way to Allergy Relief and Prevention.*
Pub Group West.

Lee, J. R. (1998). *The John R. Lee M.D. Medical Letter.* April 1998.

Levenstein, H. (1988). *Revolution at the Table: The Transformation
of the American Diet.* New York: Oxford University Press.

Lipski, L. (1996). *Digestive Wellness.* New Caanan, CT: Keats
Publishing.

Lipton, M., Marlman, R. and Nemeroff, C. (1979). Vitamins,
megavitamins therapy and the nervous system. Pp 183–246 in
Wurtman, R. J. and Wurtman, J. J. (eds). (1979). *Nutrition and
the Brain,* 3. New York: Raven Press.

Lucas, A., Morley, R., Cole, T. J., Lister G. and Leeson-Payne, C.
(1992). Breast milk and subsequent intelligence quotient in
children born preterm. *Lancet,* 339: 261–64.

Mathews Larson, J. (1998). *Seven Weeks to Sobriety: The Proven
Program to Fight Alcoholism Through Nutrition.* Fawcett.

Mathews Larson, J. (1999). *Depression Free, Naturally: Seven
Weeks to Eliminate Anxiety, Despair, Fatigue and Anger from
your Life.* Ballantine Books.

Missildine, H. (1963) *Your Inner Child of the Past.* New York:
Simon and Schuster.

Mitchell, E. A., Aman, M. G., Turbott, S. H. and Manku, M.
(1987). Clinical characteristics and serum essential fatty acid
levels in hyperative children. *Clinical Pediatrics,* 26: 40–11.

Nestle, M. (2002). *Food Politics.* Berkely, CA: University of
California Press.

Nishek, D. (2001). Challenging cancer. *Delicious Living Magazine
Annual Guide, August 2001.*

Null, G. (2001). *The Complete Encyclopedia of Natural Healing:
A Comprehensive A–Z Listing of Common and Chronic Illnesses
and their Proven Natural Treatments.* Greenwich, CT: Bottom Line
Books.

Ornish, D. (1993). *Eat More Weigh Less.* New York: Harper
Collins.

■ □ ■ □ ■

Pardridge, W. M. (1986). Potential effects of the dipeptide sweetener aspartame on the brain. Pp 199–241 In Wurtman, R. J. and Wurtman, J.J. (eds) (1986). *Nutrition and the Brain 7.* New York: Raven Press.

Pauling, L. (1968). Orthomolecular psychiatry. *Science,* 1969: 4–19.

Pawlak, L. (1999). *A Perfect 10: Phyto "New-trients" Against Cancers: A Practical Guide for the Breast, Prostate, Colon, Lung.* Emeryville, CA: Jeblar Inc.

Pererra, F. P. (1997). Environment and cancer: Who are susceptible? *Science,* 278: 1068–73.

Peskin, B. (1999). *Beyond the Zone.* Houston TX: Noble Publishing.

Pesonen E., Hirvonen, J., Karkola, K., Laaksonen, H., Viikari, J. and Akerblom, H. K. (1991). Dimensions of the coronary arteries in children. *Annals of Medicine,* 23(1): 85–88.

Pfeiffer, C. C. (1987). *Nutrition and Mental Illness: An Orthomolecular Approach to Balancing Body Chemistry.* Rochester, VT: Healing Arts Press.

Physicians Committee for Responsible Medicine. (2004) *Nutrition for Kids: A "Get Healthy" Approach to Achieving Weight Goals.* Washington D.C.: Authors.

Randolph, T. and Moss, R. (1980). *Allergies: Your Hidden Enemy.* Wellingborough, Northamptonshire, England: Turnstone Press.

Rapp, D. (1986). *The Impossible Child.* Tacoma: Life Science Press.

Recker, R. (1985). The effect of milk supplements on calcium metabolism, bone metabolism and calcium balance. *American Journal of Clinical Nutrition,* 41: 254.

Robbins, J. (1987). *Diet for a New America.* Walpol, NH: Stillpoint Publishing.

Rooizen, M. (1999). *Real Age: Are You as Young as You Can Be?* New York: Harper Collins.

Ross, J. (1999). *The Diet Cure.* New York: Viking.

Rudin, D. and Felix, C. (1996). *Omega-3 Oils: A Practical Guide.* New York: Avery Publishing.

Schlosser, E. (2001). *Fast Food Nation: The Dark Side of the All-American Meal.* Boston: Houghton Mifflin.

Schmidt, M. (1997). *Smart Fats.* Berkely, CA: Frog Ltd.

Schoenthaler, S. J. (1983). Diet and crime: An empirical examination of the value of nutrition in the control and treatment of incarcerated juvenile offenders. *International Journal of Biosocial Research,* 4(1): 25–39.

Schoenthaler, S. J. and Brier, I. (2000). The effect of vitamin-mineral supplementation on juvenile delinquency among American schoolchildren: A randomized, double-blind placebo-controlled trial. *Journal of Alternative and Complementary Medicine,* 6(1): 7–17.

Schoenthaler, S. J., Doraz, W. E. and Wakefield, J. A. Jr. (1986). The testing of various hypotheses as explanations for the gains in national standardized academic test scores in the 1978–1983 New York City nutrition policy modification project. *International Journal of Biosocial Research,* 8(2): 196–203.

Simontacchi, C. (2000). *The Crazy Makers: How the Food Industry is Destroying Our Brains and Harming Our Children.* New York: Putnam.

Sinatra, S. T. (1996). *Optimum Health: A Natural Lifesaving Prescription for Your Body and Mind.* New York: Bantam.

Smith, J. C., Holbrook, J. T. and Danford, D. E. (1985). Analysis and evaluation of zinc and copper in human plasma and serum. *Journal of American College of Nutrition,* 4: 627–638.

Smith, L. (1996). *How to Raise a Healthy Child.* New York: Evans and Co.

Steingraber, S. (1997). *Living Downstream: An Ecologist Looks at Cancer and the Environment.* Reading, MA: Addison-Wesley Publishing.

Stevens, J. (1995). *Tops and Bottoms.* Harcourt Children's Books.

Stevens, L, Zentall, S., Abate, M., Kuczek, T. and Burgess, J. (1996). Omeg-3 fatty acids in boys with behavior, learning and health problems. *Physiology and Behavior.* 59(4/5): 915–920.

■ □ ■ □ ■

Walsh, W. J. (2006). Personal communication.

Walsh, W. J., Isaacson, H. R., Rehman, F. and Hall, A. (1994). Elevated blood copper/zinc ratios in assaultive young males. *Physiology and Behaviour* 62(2): 327–29.

Werbach, M. R. (1991). *Nutritional Influences on Mental Illness: A Sourcebook of Clinical Research*. Tarzsa, CA: Third Line Press.

Werbach, M. R. and Murray, M. T. (2000). *Botanical Influences on Illness: A Sourcebook on Clinical Research*. Tarzsa, CA: Third Line Press.

Whitaker, J. (1996). There are better things than drugs for depression. *Health and Healing*, 6(11).

Wolraich, M. L. (1988) Sugar intolerance: Is there evidence for its effects of behavior on children. *Annals of Allergy*, 61(6): 58–62.

Wood, R. (1999). *The Whole Foods Encyclopedia*. New York: Penguin.

Wright, J. (1995). The story of vitamin B12. *Nutrition and Healing* 2(7).

Zimmerman, M. (1999). *The ADD Nutrition Solution*. New York: Owl Books.

Zioudrou, C., Streaty, R.A. and Klee, W.A. (1979). Opiate peptides derived from food proteins: The exorphins. *Journal of Biological Chemistry*, 254(7): 2379–2380.